Porochista Khakpour

Brown Album

Porochista Khakpour is the author of *Sick: A Memoir* and two novels. Her debut novel, *Sons and Other Flammable Objects*, was a *New York Times* Editors' Choice, one of the *Chicago Tribune*'s Fall's Best, and the 2007 California Book Award winner in the First Fiction category. Her second novel, *The Last Illusion*, was a 2014 "Best Book of the Year" according to *NPR*, *Kirkus Reviews*, BuzzFeed, *PopMatters*, *Electric Literature*, and many more. Among her many fellowships is a National Endowment for the Arts award. Born in Tehran and raised in the Los Angeles area, Khakpour currently lives in New York.

www.porochistakhakpour.com

Also by Porochista Khakpour

Sick: A Memoir

The Last Illusion

Sons and Other Flammable Objects

Brown Album

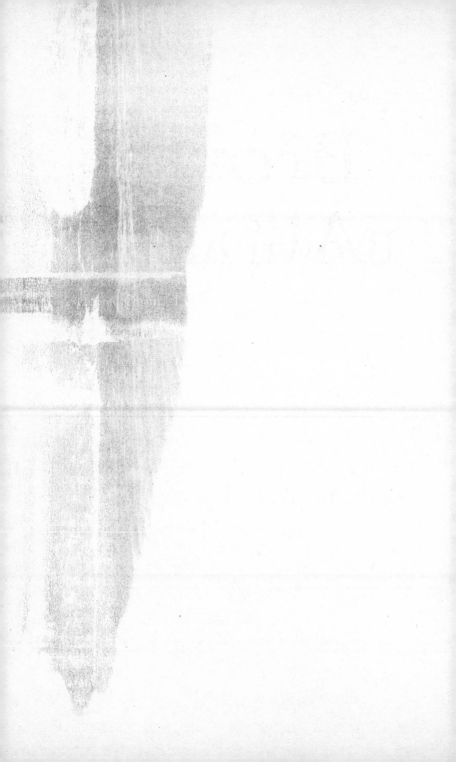

Brown Album

*

Essays on Exile and Identity

Porochista Khakpour

VINTAGE BOOKS
A Division of Penguin Random House LLC
New York

A VINTAGE BOOKS ORIGINAL, MAY 2020

Several of the essays have appeared in slightly different form in the
following publications: "A New Persian Empire" in *The New York
Times* (2012); "Revolution Days" in *The Daily Beast* (2009); "Islamic
Revolution Barbie" in *The New York Times* (2009); "Camel Ride, Los
Angeles, 1986" in *Guernica* (2011); "Another Dingbat" in *The House
That Made Me* (SparkPress, 2016); "Coming of Identity, New York
City, Late Nineties" in *Never Can Say Goodbye* (Gallery Books, 2014);
"An Iranian in Mississippi" in *Better Than Fiction 2* (Lonely Planet,
2015); "The King of Tehrangeles" in *Salon* (2011); "Blond Girls"
in *Elle* (2014); "Portrait of the Artist as a Debut Novelist" in *Scratch*
(Simon & Schuster, 2017); "Thirteen Ways of Being an Immigrant" in
The Displaced (Abrams, 2019); "Secret Muslims in the New Year" on
CNN.com (2017); "Born-Again Carnivorism" in *Aspeers* (2012);
"On Becoming a Middle Eastern–American" in *The New York Times*
(2010); "Today Is a Sunny Day" in *Granta* (2011); "The Forever
Refugee" on CNN.com (2017); "A Muslim-American in Indonesia"
in *The Lonely Planet Travel Anthology* (Lonely Planet, 2016);
"The Father of Iran's Nuclear Weapons Program" in *Vice*; and
"How to Write Iranian America" in *Catapult* (2017).

Cataloging-in-Publication Data is available at the Library of Congress.

**Vintage Books Trade Paperback ISBN: 978-0-525-56471-3
eBook ISBN: 978-0-525-56472-0**

Book design by Nicholas Alguire

www.vintagebooks.com

Printed in the United States of America
10 9 8 7 6 5 4 3 2 1

To Iranians in America: یکی بود یکی نبود

"Quite like old times," the room says.

—Jean Rhys

Contents

What follows in *Brown Album* is a great number of essays I wrote about Iranian America, mostly over the course of one decade. They are a testament to the greatest and worst experience of my life: being a spokesperson for my people, a role I never dreamed of and never asked for. This is my pigeonhole, and this is my legacy. There are no works I am better known for, no matter how many times I tell people I am, in fact, a novelist. These pieces are my bridge, and they are my cave. These works were all composed in hesitation and desperation and published to immense relief. And because of them, I was gifted a readership of those who look like me, share my story. These essays also span my career in the public eye and tell my story as a writer. Much of this book was written in tears. Most of the essays can be found online in similar and differently edited forms; some appear only in print and never made it online. But the final essay is one I wrote expansively with a goal different from that of the others: I wanted to write an essay that wasn't for publication. Visibility was the start, invisibility the end.

A New Persian Empire

In the beginning there was the word . . . *Persian*.

It was imaginary, belonging to a place that no longer exists, the realm of dusty maps and fairy tales and myths, and yet for my entire childhood it described who I was. We said "Irani" among Iranians, but among Americans, "Persian" was the name of the game. I said it because my parents said it. Only later did I sense the shame of "Iran" in an era when Iran equaled "hostage crisis" and "revolution."

Unless you are talking about one of the inhabitants of ancient Persia, *Persian* connotes the language of those from provinces where it is spoken or physical objects from modern-day Iran (just as *Oriental* refers to objects from East Asia). But while technically incorrect, *Persian* often equates with *Iranian* if you are trying to sugarcoat the name of a nationality that has been historically—and currently!—seen as controversial for too long.

I had tactics as a child: I hid inside the American costumes I wore—punk, cowgirl, starlet—and took on Persian only when I had to. Once in a while a baffled peer would ask: "But what's Persian? Aren't you from Iran?" I'd spin the wheel in my brain and let the arrow land on the many somethings, anythings, I had cobbled: *It's the label for Islamic Republic–disliking Iranians! It's what Iranians who used to be fancy prefer! It refers to a state in Iran—uh, state of mind—I mean, an actual state—yes, that's it!*

My stress was hideous. My "Oriental" best friend ("Where's Orienta?" a classmate asked her once) and my "Persian" self were perpetually rolled up into ourselves like, well, discount rugs.

As I grew older, I said *Iranian*—never mind the label's problematic past, I was concerned with owning its problematic present. In America at least, Iranian identity has never not been newsworthy, from the hostage crisis to today's Muslim ban. After the September 11 attacks I began insisting on using it over *Persian*. I didn't want to stand for more convenient euphemisms.

Little did I know 2012 would herald "The Return of the Persian." At least according to the Bravo cable channel, which that year unveiled the reality series *Shahs of Sunset*, from Ryan Seacrest Productions. The show follows a group of well-heeled friends in Los Angeles, and "Persian" is thrown around as if "Iranian" never existed. But who could blame them? It was a bad time for Iranians.

Since 9/11, we have been living in a winter of discontent after more than three decades of discontentment. Israel, Iran, and the United States play messy games of geopolitical cat and mouse and musical chairs across the ocean, and the temperature has plunged to cold-warring with sanctions that have hurt Iran's people while helping the regime. Hot-war talk hastened, but the old World War III nightmare continues to be dangled only as a threat.

For Iranians—here, there, anywhere—it means living with the tangles of neurotic defense and justification. In the endless hangover from the glory of ancient empire, we dissect old realities complicated by new contexts, we explain to others, we explain to ourselves: knotty on-and-off flings with the West; the dysfunction of church and state; extra-religious fundamentalism fronting to mask secular economic feuding. It all adds up to never-ending identity angst that perhaps only an American can understand.

Around the same time *Shahs* debuted, Asghar Farhadi's resoundingly universal 2011 feature film, *A Separation*, had artistry and coincidental timing on its side as it crept from the festival circuit to an Oscar. As the ticking of the nuclear clock grew audible, displaced hopes and anxieties clung to the film's ascent. Mr. Farhadi had said, "I think it's not only the best film, I think it's the film that has to win." And when it did, Iranians cheered on Facebook and Twitter: "We won." For once, the diaspora and homeland Iranians were connected in a uniting cause: the love of great art.

Iranian cynics, more invested than rappers in cred, piped up with their mix of hyperanalysis and haterade, jabbing while applauding. Was Mr. Farhadi, who received permission to make the film, in bed with the Iranian government? (Never mind that at one point the government pulled the plug on production after his vocal support of imprisoned filmmakers.) Was this another depiction of the unbearable difficulty of being Iranian? (Never mind that the film's meditation on divorce, Alzheimer's, and middle-class family struggles should be filed under the unbearable difficulty of being human.) Even when you win, you lose—so it goes when you are Iranian.

Perhaps Persianness can fare better? The dreaded coming out of *Shahs of Sunset* had for months spurred tweeting Iranians to tar and feather, as if no one had witnessed badly drawn reality-TV Iranians or seen a royalist-offspring comedy of errors before. Long forgotten was the 2004 E! show *Love Is in the Heir*, the goofy chronicles of the real-life Pahlavi dynasty princess Ann Claire Van Shaick and her country-music-star aspirations.

But now, in the shadow of political depression and artistic high, what does one do with *Shahs* and American specimens of Iranian descent?

When the show was announced, part of me rooted for the delicious worst: for years I've been writing about such a minstrel show, working on a novel about Iranian-American reality TV. I worried, too. But once I had watched it, I learned how much more troubling the "Persian" label proved than the been-there-done-that *Kardashian/Real Housewives/Jersey Shore* mash-up that was the show.

Plus, I wasn't above some giggles/gags of recognition here and there: GG, the show's resident "Persian princess" whose "baddest bitch" spirit is a sham to all but her; Asa, the earthy mystical urban artist with a flair for higher callings of the imitation–Erykah Badu variety; Reza, the gay Iranian real estate whiz who deals only in funny and money. Less personal but nonetheless expected is the clubby soundtrack, the racist Persian mother, and the caged tiger at a pool party.

Who could ask for anything more? Here you have it: the modern-day Persian family.

This—rest easy, Iranians!—is American culture, mainlined and snorted to overdose, specifically, the new-money culture of Westside Los Angeles, where ethnic minorities fashioned their lives in the image of their affluent white predecessors. For Iranians, this meant the eighties made them *Dynasty* extras. When GG and Asa get heated over an accusation of wearing—insult of insults—H&M, you find a generic all-American parable of new money and assimilation insanity.

In this way *Shahs* is—dare I say it?—more daunting to deconstruct than *A Separation*. Who can capture a young diaspora doing as young diasporas do: huffing freedom and crashing and burning, trying on and discarding selves made up of their parents' hand-me-down, post-traumatic stress disorder?

For many, this show has come and go, but for those of us who are members of the diaspora, facing it is in order.

For my fellow Iranian-Americans who are struggling with it: You doth protest too much, methinks. Ryan Seacrest isn't playing Columbus with Iranian America: American "shahs" have been out in malls, clubs, salons, and executive lounges around the country. The honeymoon period of immigrant invisibility is over; *Shahs* is part of the assimilation pact, as is appreciation for *A Separation*. The only way to grapple with *Shahs* is to travel back by time machine to your local royalist with a simple request: hit up a therapist before the Armani outlet.

For Iranians in Iran: Have a good laugh. Or cry. Yes, these are your cousins who were rooting for you to risk life and limb and fight the Green Revolution for them as they watched on satellite TV, sometimes the very same ones who advocated invasion of your country to liberate you. *Shahs* has at times lightly touched on the conservatism and reactionary side of the Tehrangeleno culture, but you know the full subtext.

For Persians: back in 2012, I asked a cast member, Reza, about Bravo's decision to call these Iranians Persians. His first answer danced around his hatred of the common pronunciation *EYE-ranian*, but then he said: "And things from Iran, whether they're people or objects, are all Persian. Food is Persian, rugs are Persian, cats are Persian, people are Persian. It's not because I'm ashamed or embarrassed. Mind you, I am very much more Cyrus and Darius than I am Islamic Republic."

This is an outdated Orientalist misconception. The cracked psyche is a fiction writer's dream. In short, the common yet confused explanation is also why you should not say "Persian."

For all other Americans: I asked Mr. Seacrest about Bravo's New Persianness. He replied, "As producers, we didn't impose any rules about referring to the cast one way or another, but more often than not they ended up using 'Persian' themselves."

Frances Berwick, the president of Bravo, said: "I defer to you. I don't think we have called them anything. But it's an interesting question. I don't know."

Whether these answers reflect a confused paralysis or convenient glossing, they are all tiptoeing in a time when awareness and education are critical. We Iranians are not going anywhere, but now our recognition and reception rest on your ability to elect leaders, view or not view what appears on your television and computer screens, or award accolades. What you do will decide the future for that problem child, the Persian.

Part One

*

Revolution Days

The Iranian Revolution turns forty.

I lived through it. But let's be clear: I was age one during the Iranian Revolution in 1978. While it's the one historic event that has made me more *me* than anything, I never really felt comfortable claiming to be a "child of the revolution."

For the first two and a half decades of my life, I dedicated my inner life to rehearsing for American Girl roles—working the mercilessly flat-ironed hair, generic pale olive skin, and "brown-eyed girl" for "passing" glory—while an impossible *Po-ro-chis-ta* cultivated credible Valley Girl–ese that would eventually put even Moon Unit to shame. Like many immigrants, I focused adamantly on looking forward and never back; like many hyphenates, I lived the existential confusion of a two-pronged identity.

I treasured all the pretty artifacts of old Persia: Kings Cyrus and Darius and the Persian empire; Persepolis (the ruins! Marjane Satrapi's graphic novel!); saffron-and-pistachio Persian ice cream!; rugs!; mystical Avesta chants mashed up against hokey, hooky Googoosh lyrics back to back and backward even . . . did I mention Persian cats?

But I could not approach the "Iranian Revolution." It sent shivers down my spine, making up the paragraphs of history books that I skimmed, cringing.

At twenty-five, my first novel made me go there. Like a film noir debt collector, it cornered me in a dark alley and grabbed me by the collar. I finally faced my past. This is how I learned to tiptoe around this story that is two parts my parents, one part mine.

Per annual tradition, at 9:33 p.m. on February 1—the exact date and time Khomeini's plane landed in Tehran after his fifteen-year exile—bells toll and footage of the seventy-six-year-old exiting an Air France plane plays throughout Iran. The next ten days are called the Ten Days of Dawn, highlighting the week and a half it took for Khomeini to arrive and the 2,500-year-old monarchy to buckle.

Every Iranian in the United States—particularly those who go by that purry, zhizzy *Persian*—will tell you their family was royalty or somehow connected to the Shah. But the truth is, they probably weren't and we certainly weren't. We were, however, very well off in Iran.

My parents were the youngsters of the sixties, and the young adults of seventies Tehran. They were city kids who wore their secularity like a status symbol along with their multiple degrees and their well-traveled worldliness. They were the nouveau riche who felt they had more in common with American Hollywood icons than their hired hands and their destitute families just around their corner. In 1978, after my birth, they bought a new Dodge Dart. My dad likes to say, *Trust me, it was a nice car then!* They put half the money down on a plush three-bedroom condo on Gandhi Street, in a still-tony upper-class enclave in northern Tehran. Oil production was booming and the upper echelon could feel it. It was news to them when they learned, the lowercase-R royalists, that their government was managing the economy poorly.

When the revolution hit, Dad was thirty-five and Mom twenty-eight, and they both worked on different floors of the Atomic Energy Organization of Iran (AEOI). It was a company of five thousand, where my mother's uncle Akbar Etemad was president (he would become known as "the father of the Iranian nuclear weapons program" by the international press) on top of being the country's deputy prime minister. She was an accountant, my father a researcher of theoretical nuclear physics—*Not bombs! Theory!* Dad would emphasize to me as a suspicious teenager—and they loved their jobs.

All my childhood, they described this period of their life as paradisiacal. When my brother and I got older, we were told the one exception: SAVAK, the Iranian secret police of 1957–1979. Ask any Iranian about that era's "domestic security and intelligence team," and they will laugh at the words *security* and *intelligence.* The CIA-trained SAVAK was arguably the most thuggish secret police in history, with almost limitless powers. All around Tehran, the Shah's "dissidents" disappeared at their hands or else suffered fates their friends and relatives could barely whisper about.

But hey, aside from pesky SAVAK, the seventies in Iran were a blast, my parents always insisted. Multicourse dinners out every night at the Hilton and Intercontinental, dripping in designer garb! Fetching maids in hand-me-down Chanel! My infant goods consisted of Paris-bought rabbit-fur capes and giant life-size stuffed animals and more dolls than I've ever seen outside a store. And there were the parties, constant parties. Even parties made of just the three of us, parties for my sake—parents singing and dancing to disco-fevered Googoosh at full blast. They drowned out the alien bellows that eventually filled the night air, post–10:00 p.m. curfew: the old neighbors' shouts of *Allah Akbar!* from the flanking rooftops that were replaced by the air-raid sirens of an impending eight-year war with Iraq.

Previous years' celebrations involved Iran's supreme leader Ayatollah Ali Khamenei and President Mahmoud Ahmadinejad at Khomeini's mausoleum as well as the grave sites of martyrs of the Iran-Iraq War. Ahmadinejad declared, "Today, the revolution is moving forward stronger than before!"

The Islamic Republic, its citizens, the Iranian diaspora, and my family have all undergone so many changes that commemorations today feel confusing and conflicted. The promises of 1979, and even 1989 and 1999, are no longer: Nobody's looking to the mullahs to solve homelessness anymore (Khomeini's old promise). Renewed fatwa or not, Salman Rushdie has partied out in New York for years. Khatami's two steps forward—attempts at a freer, more democratic Iran—still ended with Iran two steps back thanks to Ahmadinejad. Hassan Rouhani's election as a reformist president in 2013 has done little to bring stability to the country and little more for its perception abroad. Supreme Leader Ali Khamenei has refused to die since taking office in 1989. The Iran Nuclear Deal of 2015 remains in place even as Trump in 2018 declared that the United States would withdraw. The most startling revolutions seem to have occurred in the hearts of its participants, whether active or passive.

My father changed, too. He tiptoes around using the word *royalist*, but I grew up with more pictures of the Shah in our living room than there were photos of my relatives. Childhood classmates who came over would coo, "Wow, your dad sure got a lot of medals, right?" But my dad often likened his 1979 self to old American Republicans who crave a conservative status quo. And since my father went to grad school at MIT and my mother studied English in Britain, the West that divided the Left and the Right in Iran held neither threat nor allure for them.

Around them, everyone at AEOI was in the quintessentially Iranian proverbial faction *hizb-i bad*, or "the party of the wind"—they'd sway with the majority, whichever way they swung. But my parents remain proud of the fact that they were not persuaded by the romanticism of revolution. My father spoke quietly against the revolution in the office, as did my mother, whose last name matched the Shah's deputy prime minister. Dad's friends urged him to give up and give in, if only for safety, but he politely declined. One day he arrived at work to find that his many photos of the Shah on his desk and in the office were gone. I once asked my dad why he even went to work during this time and he laughed. "What looked worse: if you showed up or if you were in hiding?"

On February eleventh's Islamist "victory"—the Pahlavi dynasty's collapse (Iran's final ruling monarchy began in 1925, after the parliament installed former brigadier general Reza Shah Pahlavi to power, once it became clear that the previous Qajar dynasty offered no match for British and Soviet threats to Iranian sovereignty)—my father was alone against the wind of AEOI. But, by the end of the month, as beloved political leaders and key activists were executed and demonstrations grew more bloody, the first stirrings against the revolution emerged among his friends and colleagues. Some of his colleagues and friends had already left the country, and more started to flee. "I'd say it was still a velvet revolution for a while," my dad insists. "The bloodshed began once the revolution became an institution."

Every year, on the anniversary of the revolution, helicopters pour flowers on Khomeini's procession route from the airport to his first stop at the martyrs' ceme-

tery. On his plane ride back to Iran in 1979, a Western journalist had asked Khomeini how he felt when he returned to Iran after a long exile (from 1964, he lived in Turkey, Iraq, and France after Mohamed Reza Shah Pahlavi had him arrested by SAVAK for condemning what Khomeini regarded as the Shah's attempts at secularization and westernization of Iran with the White Revolution). Khomeini's answer: "Nothing." I, like many Iranians, never quite appreciated this as anything other than a brackish joke, but when I called my parents in Los Angeles to ask them how they felt about the thirtieth anniversary of the Iranian Revolution, I was taken aback by my father, who simply and genuinely answered, "Nothing."

The Iranian people and their government couldn't be more different, and neither could the Iranian diaspora of Los Angeles and Iranians in Iran then or now. The astronomically affluent, often neoconservative Tehrangelite could never meet their mainland counterparts who are either (a) too poor; (b) too proud (too in love with their country and that lifestyle to leave); (c) believers in the new regime; or (d) believers of political fickleness, who pooh-poohed the fanciful revolution phase, waiting for a counterrevolution that would set things "normal" again. Homebase Iranians and their satellite cousins now, forty years later, still do not comprehend one another. How do Irangelenos phone their Tehran aunties and dish about their Teacup Yorkies, their indoor pool, and, *oh yeah*, their pro-US invasion stance? These are people who often claim they don't even have relatives in Iran anymore.

I used to envy the glamorous-life-living Tehrangeles Iranians of Westwood, Brentwood, and Beverly Hills—a good half hour from us in quaint and sometimes cruddy Middle American Pasadena, where we were one of a few isolated lower-middle-class Iranian families. Their flash and trash made sense in L.A., with hulking hairdos, blinding bling, chichi couture, froufrou wheels, rococoocoo estates, etc. Here all the base materialism purged by the Islamists could upchuck ebulliently like a Disneyland-lit confetti-bomb blitz. They were safe.

I liked to call my family "academic aristocracy," whatever that meant. It was my way of explaining our riches-to-rags condition. They had deep accents, slim savings, and a resistance to assimilation. Like many, they believed their stay in the United States was temporary, an idea that still lives on in my father. This isolated them from Americans as well as from the overeager assimilators of the diaspora, but they still held on to some of the old glory. I shared a room with my little brother in our modest apartment in Pasadena, but I was over-dressed to the point of princess parody for school (I dreamed of Cali-staples like soccer shorts and Billabong T-shirts while I was stuffed into layers of poofy formalwear, all sent from our relatives in the European bureau of the diaspora, making daily life like a perpetual bat mitzvah). My brother and I were taught impeccable manners—to this day I neurotically affix too many *please*s and *thank-you*s to everything I say. My dad even made us supermarket caviar-butter-and-Wonder-Bread sandwiches to take to school, to remind us that "the real stuff is simply our culture." (I felt uniquely horrified until I witnessed my Chinese best friend's mortification at being picked up in her immigrant father's magnificently garish, mildly beat-up, sputtering fifties Rolls-Royce Silver Wraith.)

I became *that girl*, and luckily got it out of my system in kid-dom.

I remember the Ayatollah was not just "a nightmare" to me in the way he was to my parents—he appeared to me in horrifying dreams the way Freddy Krueger makes cameos in dreams of sleeping American children. I battled this with a total baby royalist move. The all-black-wearing white-beardo Ayatollah and his Evil Santa bad looks were canceled out by hours of pre-bedtime perusal of aesthetically pleasing Iranian figures in the numerous Pahlavi family coffee table photo books in my dad's collection. I'd swoon over Empress Farah's Jackie O chic, her honey hair and complexion, her "almost American" resplendent style. I admired their bejeweled medals and dazzling crowns and archaic castles. What's not to love about that fussy life? I decided I wanted to be like the youngest, Leila Pahlavi, with her pastel plaid shirts and carefree feathered hair that was not so unlike my own. How like a real princess she was to play down princesshood, I thought. Sadly, she grew up to be a troubled depressive and was found dead in a London hotel in 2001, having overdosed on Seconal—Marilyn Monroe and Judy Garland's final poison of choice, too.

By age seven or so, I began calling myself a "Republican," which to me smelled of royalist American style. I adopted my father's warmish support of Reagan, but with more zeal. My lexicon was littered with just-say-no-isms, I wore sweater vests à la the Keatons, I challenged students at school to heated, politically charged debates. I claimed to be prolife before I knew exactly how babies were made. And I crushed on the most American of icons, the Marlboro Man. I once got detention for telling a new male classmate with an ear piercing that he probably had AIDS.

While Ahmadinejad talked to the crowds, the obligatory "Down with America" posters bobbed before the cameras. It was a reminder that there is an air of negation and opposition in this celebration. It's the anniversary of an upheaval, not simply the birthday of an Islamic fundamentalist state.

A revolutionary expression, a protest, saved me from becoming an Iranian Ann Coulter. The event also made me demote my parents from semi-divine sages to something of the just-like-me sort.

In September 1987, our family went to one of the many Iranian protests of that era, a demonstration at the Westwood Federal Building against the visit of then president Khomeini to the United Nations and US involvement in the Iran-Iraq War. Thousands of demonstrators shouted while cars honked in solidarity (or plain mischief). I—with my head full of My Little Ponies and my new favorite show *Rags to Riches* and playground politics and first boys to crush on—truly didn't care. But suddenly, a speaker under the spotlight set himself on fire. Right in front of us. I later found out it was Iranian writer and antiwar activist Neusha Farrahi, a young man. He died two weeks later.

I could not stop thinking about him.

Around this time, I devolved into a nervous person. I started having insomnia episodes. Then I began sleepwalking. Then I developed some condition where my limbs would shake uncontrollably as if I was being electrocuted at night. And, worst of all, I began having panic attacks about death. My father tried to console me by promising me that when I got older, I would stop caring about dying so much. "Adults joke about wishing they were dead! Maybe they even mean it!" I started to pray. I prayed—truly godlessly, mimicking the generic gestures and treacly platitudes I had learned from those quivering kids perched by their windows in movies—for time to pass by *fast*.

I avoided topics about Iran and deep conversation with my parents. I mostly avoided my parents entirely until my mid-teens, when I had to study Iran in a few pages of my school's world history book. I saw a picture of someone my parents had never mentioned, a stern old man with a tragic expression. The caption explained that he was crying. My Japanese-American study buddy was intrigued— "Moooooooos Degaaaaaaaaas," she pronounced his name as if he was a ballerino MC. "What in the world happened to Mr. Mos Degas?" I shrugged, and we brought the textbook to my father. Mossadegh was a beloved former prime minister of Iran, he told us, who had been democratically elected and then ousted by a UK- and US-sponsored coup in 1953 once he tried to nationalize the Iranian oil industry. He was also *Time*'s Man of the Year—the only other Iranian who was ever given that honor was Khomeini.

Finally, I thought, an Iranian *good guy!*—and I became interested in Iran again. In the nineties, I developed that trendy fixation with "my roots," and I began obsessing over my parents' plight and seventies Iran. When the Smashing Pumpkins released the Gen X sexy 1996 hit "1979," I wormed my way into the lyrics, determined to claim 1979 revolution references (*We feel the pull / In the land of a thousand guilts!*). I dreamed up my own alternative music video renditions, and in this one I imagined my parents' journey here: my mother, played by the young Rapunzel-locked waify Cher, and my father, a burly porn-hunk Tom Selleck. In reality, my mother was more *Funny Girl*–era Streisand, while my dapper lanky-nerd Dad resembled Obama. I saw them running through a vast barren sci-fi *Land of the Lost* landscape full of bloodthirsty overgrown lizards, but somehow by the chorus finale, they were beamed up all shimmying, hustling, bumping in Halston and Qiana atop a *Solid Gold* platform in glittering *le-freak*-ing America.

But the true story is that they ended up in one of many one-bedroom moldy and roach-infested apartments in the more downtrodden suburbs of Los Angeles's East Side, many worlds away from other Iranians, whether they be of their homeland or in the city's opulent West Side.

Who knows if it took that painful transition and its endlessly sobering realities over the next few years to really change us? My father's change was the most drastic: a complete departure from right to left by the post 9/11 era. It seemed like it happened overnight. Dad—who used to champion the lunatic-charm Americana of his beloved wise-cracking musical-belting Danny Kaye, who used to glorify this land of good ol' American apple pies and upstanding Puritan ethics—went from a guy whose only criticism of the

United States had been President Carter's failure to back the Shah when he fell, to a very West-wary liberal. My brother, with his Near Eastern studies training, started preaching to us three completely confused Iranian immigrants. He convinced me to later shriek *Orientalist!* at grad-school friends who thought I should put more names of spices in the titles of my stories. My brother converted my dad into a left-wing, Trader Joe's–frequenting *Air America*–addicted Naderite—my dad, who dubbed me "Dubya" when I dared to ask for a dialogue around his *No More Prisons!* mantra. You can't quite equate today's Democratic and Republican allegiances with Iranian political affinities, but this is like a libertarian swinging to communism.

But my mother, most royal of us all in blood, had trouble giving up her memory of old Iran. The practice of wearing veils infuriated her, but nothing was worse than remembering all they had left behind in *her* golden era. "It was like heaven," she described, in contrast with her first weeks in Europe: "I remember I had a hard time at the butcher in Paris because I didn't know the English or French word for 'beef,' and he actually made me draw a picture of a cow! Of course, he knew from the beginning what I meant—the jerk wanted to flirt!" And in contrast with her first moments on US soil, where a smirking customs officer rolled his eyes at their visas and hissed, "Your country holds our people hostage and you have the guts to come *here*?"

The Ten Days were almost up, but still there were rallies and speeches, film festivals, gallery openings,

special exhibits, and more. In the streets everything was lit red, white, and green. This was a big nation-wide party.

My first birthday party fell on the night of January 16, 1979, the day the Shah left Iran. A year and a half later, he died in Egypt in exile from complications of non-Hodgkin's lymphoma. That evening my father was rushing from one of the poshest bakeries in town, where he had picked up a giant rabbit-shaped chocolate cake, when he found himself stuck amidst shouting crowds. He shielded the cake box as people threw candy into crowds, danced with their kids, embraced friends and family, congratulated strangers. When he finally made his way to our home, our relatives and their kids were hovering over oblivious-infant me. My father remembers feeling scared, he remembers adults muttering grimly about the celebration outside, he remembers some worried faces and some vexed sighing, but our little party went on in spite of that other party outside. My mother remembers looking at her little birthday girl and without the slightest hint of exasperation laughing it all off. *That whole thing will blow over, blow over soon enough, just wait.*

Islamic Revolution Barbie

In the days leading up to Barbie's cougariffic fiftieth birthday, most everyone had a story to tell. Mine begins in 1958 in one of the world's oldest continuously inhabited cities, Hamadan, Iran, and it begins with my mother, then just a small girl, and Barbie's international predecessor and antithesis: the porcelain baby doll.

My mother used to break her porcelain baby dolls, a luxury among her friends, who grew up with rag dolls sewn together by mothers and sisters. One day my grandmother, the teacup-size trophy wife of the president of the National Iranian Oil Company of Hamadan, took my mother to the local toy store in search of a replacement. To their horror, there were no dolls to be found.

She asked a clueless male cousin en route from Europe

to bring my mother a new doll. When it arrived, the new doll was everything the other doll was not: here was a foot-long fussy thing, half the mass and a quarter of the weight of the old clunky ceramic suckling. Some parts were molded (earrings, lashes, breasts); others simply painted on (made-up face, polished fingernails, side-scoping eyes), and the doll wore grown-lady garb. It was the German Bild Lilli doll—the prototype that Ruth Handler used to create the American Barbie in 1959—the postwar, sugar-daddy-mongering vixen of German comic strips.

My mother was puzzled. How do you play with this? It's a woman, not a baby! My grandmother had to take Lilli and my mother to the store, where the old dolls were restocked, and so my mother gave her European doll up for yet another breakable, but round and cradle-able, infant, the type my mother could more comfortably mother.

Twenty years later, when Cher was her icon, my mother finally *got* Barbie. In my infancy in Tehran, I was awarded my first, a beaming blond Malibu or SuperStar Barbie decked out in a disco metallic bikini. My mother was in love, and as soon as I was old enough to register playthings, so was I. From then, it was perpetual Barbie season in the Khakpour household.

That is, until we had to flee Iran. When my family left Tehran at the advent of the Iran-Iraq War in 1980, we left behind an entire room full of expensive toys; the casualties included my beloved Barbie posse.

The transition to another life was made easier for me, I think, by the realization that it was a small world. Barbies were to be found everywhere. On one of our first days as refugees in Paris, I shrieked my family to a dead halt in front of Galeries Lafayette, the famous department store. There, in the window display, was Pink & Pretty Barbie. My mother, who was trying to save every penny for an uncertain future, turned to my grandmother for help buying dolls once again. I was elated; Barbie was eternal and universal no matter where we were.

Once we settled in Los Angeles, I was allowed, over the years, to build up a battalion with Great Shape, Dream Date, and Rocker Barbies, with some pink Vettes and a Dream House. But toward the end of my time in elementary school, just when I was starting to look at myself in the mirror, Barbie started to make me feel uneasy. I began Sharpie-ing the hair on my Barbies black to look like mine and calling them by Persian names: Bahareh, Banafsheh, Skippareh. I even attempted to "tan" Peaches 'n Cream Barbie's skin for hours one day, praying for her lotion-slathered skin to turn brown like mine, which it never did. I realized then that the one thing worse than being a foreigner was being a foreigner who was a *girl*.

Just as Barbie was coming to mean less and less to me, she was coming to mean more and more to the folks back in Iran. In the still shiny and new Islamic Republic, Barbie was spotlighted as a national threat of Jane Fonda magnitude. Wary of Western influences and her nation-corrupting pulchritude, the Institute for the Intellectual Development of Children and Young Adults developed sibling dolls named Sara and Dara to compete with the influence of Barbie. They were

Muslim versions with headscarves and prayer books in lieu of convertibles and boom boxes. The government raided stores that carried Barbies—but this mostly resulted in black stickers on the packaging to hide the dolls' calamitous contours.

In April 2008, Iran's prosecutor general, Ghorban-Ali Dorri Najafabadi, warned Iranians about the culturally "destructive" consequences of importing Barbies and again promoted Sara and Dara as alternatives. And yet at three times the price and mostly a black-market moll, Barbie reigns supreme as the doll of choice in the Islamic Republic of Iran.

In fact, Iran may be the only place where Barbie still captures young hearts and inflames adult minds. A hundred careers, fifty nationalities, forty pets, a billion pairs of shoes, and fifty thousand makeovers later, Barbie came and conquered in the last place she could. Her sales in the United States have been falling for years.

Why did my Barbies end up dismembered, naked, pierced, and slashed in the toy-dregs mausoleum of dusty closet crates? Girls do this, according to research from the University of Bath, as a "rite of passage." I, though, felt true ire—by my pre-teenage years I was sure Barbie was in cahoots with my mother: impossibly beautiful plus an extra dose of bossy, someone who chased me around the house with lipstick before an "event."

For one brief phase in my life, though, she got to me. By the final years of my teens, still freshly in New York, without family, without an Iranian friend in sight, I took to filling myself in and out, like a coloring book. My makeup palette turned multichromatic and mad, and for exercise I raved at nightclubs: Patricia Field stilettos, iridescent body shimmer, sparkly hot pants, and a sky-high Afro—I was all hot pink, pleather and prattle.

My mother asked me, that summer: *What have you become?*

My life during daylight hours was constrained to a crummy cubicle in an office where I was the sole "ethnic person." One day I found myself at lunch with the usual middle-aged, disgruntled coworkers, all women. One hairy-eyeballed my big container of dressing-less salad and Diet Sunkist Orange— either that or my gold glitter French manicure—and muttered "Persian Barbie" under her breath.

She left quickly before I could jump out of my seat and give her the hug of my life.

Camel Ride,
Los Angeles, 1986

It had come down to this: a camel ride.

It was the middle of the eighties, and I was at the Los Angeles Zoo, a place I had never been before. The air was dusty and soft-celled, the sky was orange and cloudless, our faces were a light lavender, and my hair was a glossy black bowl, my body too thin and sloppily tucked into overalls. This is what the matte photos tell us today. There is a picture of me attempting to embrace an all-white goat in the petting zoo; another of me in front of one indifferent giraffe; and one where I'm trying to force a straw from a supersize cup into my little brother's nose and the blurry hand at the edge is trying to stop me. It belongs to my father.

There is no picture of us with the camels. That is only, only, only in my head, where it doesn't belong, either.

It was our lucky day, in the middle of a week, a school day our father let us get off. He was working that coming weekend, a fact we did not know; again and again, he said it was because he loved us so much, which he reminded us of on the way there and on the way to everywhere we went. We went to see the lions, which he reminded us appeared on the Iranian flag, which *is* still our flag, and the polar bears, which looked out of place in the sunshine. But he assured us they were fine and told us that they loved the climate that Los Angeles and Tehran shared. We saw the monkeys, who were sleeping all except for one, who entertained the laughing masses by regurgitating whatever food he kept trying to eat over and over. This my father did not like—*what is the meaning of this, of him?*—but he tolerated us standing there for our sake. There were animals we wanted to leave and animals we did not want to leave.

There was one breed of animal in particular that we wanted to leave. They frolicked behind a yellow-and-maroon sign, a few simple words announcing conveniently a question that felt more like an interrogation: WHO DOESN'T WANT TO RIDE A CAMEL?

We didn't want to. My father pointed out that one camel could take all three of us. How fortunate for us. He told us we didn't have to be scared. All the other kids were loving it.

We weren't scared. I wasn't scared, rather, as I wasn't at all thinking about my little brother, although he was suddenly quiet enough for me to think he was with me on this one. Time started to move slowly. My vision focused on myself, my father, and that camel. Something, I felt, had to be done to keep us from taking the camel ride.

My father said, "Are you ready? Come on, everyone! This is what you've been waiting for!"

But what we'd been waiting for was a place where we could be like everyone else, rid of a certain yellow-and-maroon script, rid of rides on the backs of things or just the idea of us riding on the back of that thing.

We two children stood there, frozen, shamed, butts of a cruel joke. Only I looked at my father, straight in the eye, though he was already counting dollar bills, asking my mother to get in line for us.

✻

We were only a few years into our arrival in America, a place I attempted to call home, even though my parents warned me that it was all temporary. My first memories were my last memories of Iran: first, an old man at a party with much dancing sitting with me—a relative, perhaps—talking and talking and suddenly stirring his tea with a finger; the next, false air raids in the night sky of Iran, empty threats from Iraq-side, a circle of beautiful pink lights in the black night sky, a thing of beauty to me, even in my mother's shaking arms.

I learned English watching *The Twilight Zone*. I filled our quiet home with the magical incantation: "You're traveling through another dimension, a dimension not only of sight and sound, but of mind. A journey into a wondrous land whose boundaries are that of imagination. That's the signpost up ahead. Your next stop . . . the Twilight Zone!"

I also learned English by imitating kids on the playground of my preschool, a twilight zone I was thrown into early.

They said bad words, I said bad words, and I went home and repeated the bad words to my parents. Usually it was okay because they didn't know what the words meant, either, but sometimes they did and then a huge sadness would fill the room and not leave until the blabber of the TV interrupted and shook off its weight.

I loved this country with the lukewarm, watery, neither-here-nor-there love that you bestow upon any country when it's the only country you know. I accepted it and never, until much later, considered that it might not accept me.

❋

The camel has a nameplate on its blanket. The plate says its name is Scheherazade. An echo: the name of a relative of mine is Shahrzad, but I think no relation. My father, however, points it out and laughs loudly. My mother, whose relative it is, smiles weakly, more bored than anything. Where is my mother? I wonder. It's a question I often have. She is off in the Sears catalogue, in *One Life to Live*, in herb and kidney bean and lamb stew for dinner tonight, in laundry and dishes.

I look to my brother, who looks lost in the endless empty fantasies of zoo life. It is clear I am alone with my concern for the situation.

There is another camel named Latte and another camel named Coco, but I see Scheherazade alone, and Scheherazade alone sees us.

❋

I became good at becoming one of them. For the most part. One thing I realized was that to become one of them, you can't just think of them as *them*. You think of them as people, which is odd and less obvious and more exhausting than it sounds. Which type of *them* would you like to be? Take a role. There was the teacher's pet, the prettiest girl, the class clown, the fastest runner, the shyest kid, the genius, the most crazy. There were two roles that appealed to me: the weird one and the bad girl. I was terrifically suited for the first. My clothing style in the first grade was a compromise of dependence and independence—I wore whatever overdressed thing my mother wanted but added a few items of my own, those fluffy dresses she adored topped with my cowboy hat or neon soccer socks or a scarf tied around my head as a bandanna. Kids always commented on how weird I looked. I started to say weird things, make jokes that made no sense even to me and noises that were otherworldly, and took on a faraway look in my big—too big—eyes. During recess I drew instead of played, which was also a weird thing to do. I hung out with teachers more than other students: weird. Even a teaching assistant called me a weirdo for tagging along with her so often. I displayed the contents of my lunches from home: a gray mottled eggplant dip that smelled "like carpet," I declared, beating them to it even though I loved few things more than kashkeh bademjan and the bright yellow rice pudding with a heart in cinnamon, sholeh zard, which I also loved and pretended was made of plastic for their sake. They wrinkled their noses and some shrieked and even moved away while I smiled. Weird, weird, weird.

I was less suited for the bad girl image, but I wanted it badly. Movies told me that another way to be different was to be a villain. When it came time to try out for roles in my elementary school's production of *Dorothy and the Rainbow Connection*—a more-suitable-for-a-kiddie, low-budget version of *The Wizard of Oz*—I knew exactly who I wanted to be. All the popular and pretty girls auditioned for Dorothy, Glinda, and even Toto, but I wanted to play the Wicked Witch of the East. My teacher looked at me, amused. She told me, "You're too good to be a bad witch. At best you could be a good witch." I took this badly, as I did other experiences where adults tried to discourage me—my piano teacher, frustrated by my slow learning, said my hands were better suited for pottery; my ice skating teacher complained that I dragged my left foot oddly, until she asked me to withdraw, worried I had some kind of *condition*.

But these were my only conditions: badness, weirdness.

I tried out for the bad witch defiantly, in front of my teacher, who smiled as if she had forgotten what she advised. I tried out and I failed. I did not get a lead, but I did get a one-liner. I played Dorothy's cousin Laurie, a made-up character, who in one line was to catalogue all the food they had at a particular Kansas reunion: fried chicken, biscuits, gravy, mashed potatoes, sweet potato pie, . . . etc. All the foods I never ate, foods that a future self might argue could, with the right lens, be seen as weird and bad.

❋

Scheherazade is being fed a handful of something that looks like grass. It's hard to say if Latte and Coco are given the same stuff, but one has to assume they are. One has to assume.

※

"It will soon be over," my mother is saying, with a light hand on my shoulder.

Where is my mother? My mother was the one who was always home, but where was she? Why could I never get a solid grasp on her? I thought if I could only remember when she was pregnant with my brother, five years ago—big like those balloon mothers with babies inside them on TV—then she'd be substantial for me. It's possible even then I'd think of her as a vessel for my little brother. She was already something of that to me when she wasn't my father's wife or my grandparents' daughter. Or Shahrzad and the others' cousin. When will she be my mother? I wondered.

I never acted bad enough to make her mad or worry, which my father and brother seemed to do. But was I good enough for her? She tried to make cupcakes once, her first attempt. She passed the bowl of batter to me. I looked at it, confused. She said, "You shouldn't eat too much of this. It can make you fat. You can become like those fat Americans." I didn't eat any of it; I never became a fat American, not even as I got older. She looked down at the pasty mess and sniffed it and put the bowl in the sink. "Anyway, Iranians can be fat, too, remember. We're no better than anyone else, no matter what your dad says. . . ."

❊

Dad is saying, "It is time! It is time! Who doesn't want a camel ride, indeed?!" He is saying that, as immigrants are prone to, so decorously in English, while otherwise casually rattling it off in Farsi. And this is the worst part for me: everyone hears him in his accent—horribly Middle Eastern—getting excited about a camel ride.

I am staying put, looking not at him but at my mother, who looks weak and bored. She finally points at me—but it's not quite at me, I realize. It is over me; it is at him, my father. She is telling me to go to him.

But my father no longer looks like my father. He looks like a Middle Eastern man I don't know. He looks like a sheikh, a terrorist, a sultan, a mullah, a dervish, a *camel jockey*.

How do I know that term? I do not know how I know that term.

"Are you coming?" he is saying, still in English. "The camel is waiting!"

I shake my head.

"Be a good girl, come on!" he is saying.

But I'm a bad girl. I am the worst girl. I want nothing to do with that camel. But I don't say that, of course. By the time he gets to me, I say what I usually say when I am in a predicament, something that is not altogether untrue.

"I can't do it," I say. "I'm suddenly very sick. Help."

❊

I never needed to ask who my father was. I knew him well.

He was the one of us who should have been the most worried. Jet-black hair, dark-brown skin. His eyes were all pupil. He looked the way others imagined he would look.

My mother had hair she dyed reddish blond and light skin to go with it. They said she looked like a non-lead actress from *Dynasty*, a show I didn't know then, but a name I heard mentioned around her cousins, who liked to flatter her over and over, maybe in attempts to make her more present. But she was like those fair women on TV, in supermarkets, outside waiting for their blond children—like lemon and ice and water and snow and winter. She was barely there.

My brother had her light eyes and light curls, as if she dyed it so much that the lightness took permanence in him. This will pass, they said. Young kids have lighter hair that darkens as they grow older. But when I looked at old photos of myself, my hair was black, black like my father's. The sun alone made my hair play brown.

I was a lot like him, they also said. This embarrassed me. I wanted no part of him. I didn't want to be like her, either. I wanted to be unlike them and everyone else, too. I wanted to be the girl with no bubble beside her name, nothing to fill in. I wanted to be something altogether different, but instead I was like him.

And he was unmistakable. And just as you'd imagine, he had the temper, too. Everything about him was loud, even his laughter. He played native music too loudly, he prayed with all his might, and when he said *my country*, he did not mean this one. He was the one who told us over and over that we wouldn't be in this country for long. It took me a long time to realize that he was often wrong and that I should not take him so seriously.

But at seven, when he said *camel ride*, I didn't know what my outs were. There was no reasoning with him, I thought.

And so I told him I was sick and I thought I was sick—thought myself into being sick—and I *was* sick. I felt sick, I was sick, he had no choice now but to accept it and go ahead with the camel ride anyway, bad father of a bad girl that he was.

❋

He puts a hand on my forehead and says I feel cool. He calls my mother over and she tries it, too.

"She is okay," she says, staring off somewhere, somewhere far, far away.

She hands over my brother, who is smiling at the sky.

"Don't stare into the sun," my father reminds him. That is in Farsi. In English he adds, "Who doesn't want to ride a camel, right? Right?"

My brother is in. He's fallen. There is nothing I can do.

❋

I never felt any jealousy for my brother. He could have the cute, the adorable, the sweet, the good. At four, he knew to hug and kiss everyone. He said *I love you* like it was just another nursery rhyme. He had a monopoly over things I didn't want, the good and the normal.

Our worlds rarely intersected. I read to him while he

played with toy trucks. When he cried for a toy at the drug-store, I pretended he didn't exist. Once or twice, I was asked to watch him when my mother went out while my dad was working, and it was too much like nothing. Neither he nor I were ever in danger when we were alone.

But we were sometimes in danger when they were with us. With my mother, because she was never there. With my father because of things like this, how things come down to things like this.

❊

His hand, big and sweaty, is around my wrist. His other arm is around my brother. My mother is behind us, waiting, wav-ing, even as she looks down at the pavement.

I don't know if I am doing it on purpose, breathing loudly to remind him he is being negligent of his sick daughter, or if I am actually gasping for air, sick as I am.

We're second in line. Second and last. The line ends with us. It is, as I suspected, not popular at the moment for anyone to ride camels.

My father finally notices my upset. "What's wrong, liver?" he says. Except *liver* in Farsi means "dear." "Why so sad? This is a great opportunity. So much fun!"

I look down and put my hand over my heart. It is not exaggerated; my heart is actually pounding, as if it's knocking against my chest. Let me out of here, it says.

"I just don't want to ride the camel," I say. "And I'm sick."

My father laughs too loudly. "You are afraid, is that it? There is nothing to be afraid of!"

I shake my head.

"Then what is it? You're not sick, trust me!"

What can I say? I would say, *Father, I don't want to be taken for what I inevitably think others will take this as, a group of Middle Easterners here—and just a few years after these guys were selling "Fuck Iran" buttons in supermarkets, something I will learn about much later—Father, but you must have known, or did you not, did you choose not to know?—a group of Middle Easterners, about to get on the back of, of all animals, a camel, the camel being the animal they associate with us, what they take us as, camel jockeys, haven't you heard, haven't you heard, and don't ask me how I've heard. . . . Father, why would we put ourselves in that position? Isn't there a danger in that? And if not real danger, then isn't there danger in exposing us to too much public humiliation? For even if it isn't on their lips, it certainly is in their eyes, and I swear, I can read their eyes—*

"I just hate camels, that's all," I tell him in the end, all I can think of saying.

And for a second there is something scary I see in his eyes. "There is nothing to hate. It's just an animal, that's all. What is there to hate?"

I don't say anything, and then it's our turn.

We ride the camel. My father behind us, clutching both me and my brother in front of me, all three of us silent as a blond woman with a big smile, with eyes shielded behind big sunglasses, walks Scheherazade around the riding area. *A journey into a wondrous land whose boundaries are that of imagination*, it is not. I expect the ride to take an eternity, but it lasts the five or so minutes they advertise. It feels like five minutes on top of a camel in the sun, against your father and your brother, nothing more or less.

Then we are down, and my mother and father get into a fight because she forgot to take a picture and my father wonders how in the world she could, when she has been so good about it all day. And then my brother has a fit by the ice-cream stand, which is all out of the particular type of ice cream he wanted, and I put my hands over my ears to block him out and he pushes me, harder than I know he had in him, and I lose my balance and topple into a vat of cactus.

The rest of our time is spent in the zoo's hospital, where a kind old lady with tweezers plucks out the needles stuck in my skin, one by one.

My father is asking me if I am in pain over her shoulder in Farsi and I don't answer him. My mother is outside entertaining my brother, who is finally eating the ice cream he wanted, bought from another stand, a reward for his wrongdoing.

And the old lady is trying to get me to speak, too. She asks if I did anything fun. My father finally interjects, "Well, we took a camel ride."

All those needles in me don't even affect me. I say nothing; I let him have it.

The old lady chuckles. "How brave of you," she says to me and just me.

I look her straight in the eye, questioning.

"You fucking dune goons," she goes on. "Why don't you go back to your country?"

My heart is pounding. Did she really say that?

No.

She said, "How brave of you. I would have been nervous up there, on a thing like that."

I nod. How do I tell her I was? That I was so sick I could die?

By the time the needles are out of me, I am a grown woman, old even, old as the old lady herself. I won't be surprised except by the beautiful things in life, of which there are fewer than I would have thought. Love is hard, acceptance harder, belonging still hardest. Home is still nothing, who has time for home and all the wondering about its wondrous whereabouts.

That orange and lavender day spent among animals is nothing, just a day—as he would say, what is there to hate?

Another Dingbat

1. Tropical Gardens

Here is *1675 Amberwood Drive, South Pasadena, California 91030*, the apartment complex I grew up in. The first apartment we lived in was No. 31, a third-floor unit on the northwest end of the building, two bedrooms and one bathroom for the four of us. I spent first grade to eleventh in those rooms. Then we moved into No. 19, which was in the southeast end, two stories, with three bedrooms and two bathrooms. Up until the age of seventeen, I shared a room with my brother, but my final year of high school I got to have the first room of my own since I was an infant.

The complex was all cream on the outside—perhaps simply off-white with time—with dark green trimmings. The words *Tropical Gardens* were dashed off in the sort of cursive you might find on the cover of a fifties homemaking magazine or adorning a cake. Built in 1957, it wasn't even thirty years old by the time we arrived in 1984. Because of a parking garage beneath them, all the units had overhanging balconies, which felt luxurious to me and were my favorite feature of our home, especially since we had no yard. But it also felt to me like the building was on stilts. I remember worrying about whether it could survive a big earthquake, even though I lived through two big ones while in that complex. The most powerful I'd experienced was the Northridge earthquake of 1994, on the day of my sixteenth birthday. Our building suffered no real damage, which, I remember, shocked me at the time.

The carpet in our first apartment there was a light brown, the color of coffee with milk, made of a terrible matted thin fur, like the coat of my poodle years later. In the second apartment, the carpet was thicker, shaggier, a swirl of dark brown, beige, and white, like the melted remains of a chocolate sundae. The ceilings were short and plain in both, but there were ample windows—the first had a view of the railroad and the War Memorial Building and a mansion I made up countless stories about; the second faced out on Amberwood Drive, a quiet street, only disturbed occasionally by a passing car, a dog walker, a skater, a leaf blower.

These apartments were the only homes of my upbringing, since I don't remember our apartment in Tehran or the temporary homes along our way to the United States, like our first American apartment in Alhambra, also small and dingy and nothing to boast about.

My parents chose South Pasadena for its solid public school system. Everyone says: "You move to South Pasadena for the schools." The walls of our living room were covered in books, shelf upon shelf, and the yellow spines of the *National Geographics* my father tried so hard to collect as a subscriber. There were also multiple sets of secondhand encyclopedias, framed illustrations of old Persian empire relics, photos of us, vases, bad couches. At one point, my parents bought a red, white, and blue plaid couch—they claimed they loved it, but I knew it was considerably marked down on sale. I couldn't stand to look at it.

It doesn't surprise me that my parents finally convinced themselves that they'd never return to Iran. They bought a condo in nearby Glendale, where it was cheaper and where I visit now and from where I remember where I once lived. I like to describe that home as "a kitschy sixties apartment district in the part of South Pasadena all the rich kids called *the South Pasadena projects*." For most, to live in South Pasadena meant you lived in a home, a Craftsman, a Victorian, but definitely not an apartment.

2. Dingbats

1998: Vivian, Natasha Lyonne's teenage character in *Slums of Beverly Hills*, knows what dingbats are. "*Casa Bella*, another dingbat—that's what they're called. *Dingbats*. Two-story apartment buildings featuring cheap rents and fancy names. They promise the good life but never deliver."

1999: *LA Weekly*, Mark Frauenfelder wrote a column called "How I Came to Love the Dingbat":

> You couldn't make an uglier building if you tried. Los Angeles is full of dingbats—boxy two-story apartments supported by stilts, with open stalls below for parking. (Their name is likely to have been coined by architect Francis Ventre while he was lecturing at UCLA in the early '70s.) Thousands of the inexpensive 16-unit structures were built in the late '50s and early '60s to accommodate the huge number of people moving to Southern California. Forty years later, the smog-stained, sagging dingbats are still here, and have become as much a part of the LA landscape as medfly traps and on-ramp pistachio vendors. . . .
>
> Recently, my interest in dingbats swelled even more after becoming exposed to the contagious enthusiasm of Lesley M. Siegel, an LA artist who has photographed over 2,000 of the signs that are sometimes attached to the outside of dingbats. With names like The Belvan, The Hayworth House, The Riviera Palms, The South Pacific, The Unique, and The UnXled, these painted, jigsaw-cut wood signs have been a source of fascination for Siegel even

before she started photographing them in 1990. Spelled out in loopy script or whimsical lettering, the names provide look-alike dingbats with a sense of individuality. More importantly, like incense, they mask the acrid tang of life in an oversized shoebox with an air of relaxed, tropical, exotic, or well-heeled splendor.

If you comb through the Internet you will find a shocking number of "in praise of the dingbat" articles, particularly from the nineties.

3. The Raymond

The South Pasadena projects weren't all dingbats, or at least it didn't start out that way. Pasadena was settled by Midwesterners who wanted to have temperate winters in the Wild West—mainly the ailing, the elderly, the rich. My dingbat and all the adjacent dingbats were built on the site of a major hotel that attracted dignitaries and luminaries from across the state and country. Raymond Hill, as the neighborhood is known now, was once Bacon Hill and contained only the Raymond Hotel. It took three years and more than two hundred fifty workers for wealthy hotelier Walter Raymond to build: fifty-five acres of South Pasadena's Bacon Hill were blasted and flattened for a four-story Second Empire–style building with two hundred guest rooms, forty-three bathrooms, forty water closets, and a 104-foot-tall tower. It opened its doors on November 17,

1886, with an inaugural ball of 1,500 guests, which the *Los Angeles Times* called "perhaps the most extensive social affair in the history of the county."

It was Southern California's leading resort hotel until Easter Sunday 1895, when one of the Raymond's eighty chimneys landed on the hotel's wood roof and burned the structure down. It took six years for Raymond to rebuild and reopen the Raymond, this time with double the rooms and more amenities. The Great Depression took the hotel down for the second and final time. It was foreclosed in 1931 and was demolished in 1934. After a few attempts at the construction of various housing developments on the former lot of the Raymond Hotel, the fifties saw the neighborhood reincarnated in its current form: dingbat life.

4. Raymond Hill

These days, when I reflect on my time growing up in Pasadena, I think, *So much happened there.* When I lived there, I thought nothing at all happened. I can see myself at seven, hunched over my white Kmart desk, with Disney curtains drawn above me, and a pile of books I could barely read at my side—a paperback of a Shakespeare play, secondhand guides to literature, a dictionary, a thesaurus—a red pen with ink that smelled like strawberries in my hand. I scrawled novel after novel in careful cursive. It was practice for a future I had imagined for myself in this faraway land called New York City, where I knew writers lived.

I also can see myself crying into a jeweled compact my mother had given me, horrified by the ugliness of my reflection, especially when faced with my mother, the great beauty.

I can still see my father's violent fits.

I see the shame of sharing a room with a brother who was five years younger than me while I was in my teens.

I see my Casio keyboard, my Walkman, the record player, the mixtapes, the boom box, and what little escape contemporary music could provide for me.

I think of the droughts, the El Niño rains, the earthquakes, and those eighties serial killers never too far away.

And I recall my first natural disaster in America. I'd lived through the unnatural one, war, in Iran. But the great fire of October 1984 happened right outside my bedroom window at Ole's Home Center hardware store. It killed a handful of people; for years I believed it *was* somewhat natural—an electrical issue compounded by October heat—but it turned out to be the work of a serial arsonist who was also a prominent fire investigator, who was linked to the crime ten years later when federal prosecutors found he'd written novels that were confessions of sorts. They detailed his hand in several major fires of the eighties.

I think of walking to and from school (a subject of shame for us South Pasadena project kids, like eating cafeteria food instead of a lovingly packed lunch), and I think of how much I cried in the bedroom, in the bathroom, and perhaps most of all on that balcony, which felt glorious as it precariously hovered in a sort of heaven—a smog-filled one; I remember the constant haze and smog that enclosed my youth. The sky looked as beige as our carpets, and we looked like everyone, anyone you might want to transpose on us, depending on who you were and what you knew. In the world of our ding-bats, so much undefined and so beautifully so—there were no references for our reality on television or on the radio. It was maybe the first and last time I got to belong to nothing in particular.

Coming of Identity, New York City, Late Nineties

Out of the over half a million Iranians who lived in Los Angeles at that point—representing the most substantial chunk of the four million Iranians of the diaspora—our family of four comprised half the Iranian population of South Pasadena, California. There was one other Iranian family apart from ours, but I was the only Iranian not only in my grade but in the whole elementary school, middle school, and high school. Westwood's Tehrangeles, where the overwhelming majority of California's Iranians, rich and proud, set up their sparkling shops, was forty-five minutes and a whole world away. Only two or three other kids in the school accounted for all the Middle Eastern students in general. There were the popular, well-dressed Egyptian sisters, one older and one younger than me; a wild Lebanese girl who claimed to be a model; and the Syrian cross-country bro with the lisp. I never exchanged more than an *excuse me* with any of them in the halls, and as far as I could tell, I was invisible to them.

My dad tried to make up for this by telling me they were all Iranian, but self-hating ones who were too ashamed to openly bond with me. His explanation for the mass migration of Iranians to Los Angeles is one I still use today: the climates of Tehran and Los Angeles are identical. I imagined Iran of the 1970s to be a place of palm trees and glittering gold and made-up ladies draped in jewels and trendy clothes, so I never questioned the portmanteau, Tehrangeles's, logic. I just knew *those* Iranians—most Iranians—who flocked to Westwood, Beverly Hills, Brentwood, and Santa Monica would not have accepted us and our little city of Pasadena, just a half hour away. NASA Jet Propulsion Laboratory and Caltech eccentrics, Rose Parades and Victorian homes, and the first Trader Joe's were just not the stuff Iranians were made of.

I dreamed of giving up crazy, conflicted California and getting myself as far away as possible. New York City had the shimmer of an unofficial American capital, a place where every type of human on earth converged—and not just all sorts, but the chosen ones of the all sorts. The song said if you could make it there you could make it anywhere, and I believed it. I was about to start applying to colleges and figured this was my chance to escape.

I researched colleges and picked out obvious Ivies. One school I had never even heard of chose me. I received an informational pamphlet that sold me with a motto: "You Are Different. So Are We."

Sarah Lawrence's obvious clairvoyance made it the place

to go. Plus, they boasted a stellar creative writing program, and creative writing had been my first love, one I had never had the chance to explore in an academic setting—my schools didn't offer even a unit in English class that asked students to explore writing their own poetry and prose. I had never met a creative writer in my life. My early Internet chat-room dabblings (O AOL! O Prodigy! O dial-up!) consisted of searching for everything New York City and ended up leading to my interest in beat culture and the still-thriving state of the East Village in the nineties. Sarah Lawrence was a place teeming with writers and artists, renegades and mavericks, lesbians and vegans, rockers and rappers. I thought it could be a place where I could pile on identities as if they were pizza toppings, cheap and fast and easily picked off, but hopefully so amply loaded that who I actually was could be, for once, truly obscured.

It charged so much for tuition—at that point Sarah Lawrence ranked as the most expensive college in America—that it could afford to cover mine. This is what sold my parents, who initially imagined I would go to a University of California school. I waved my Hearst Scholarship at them, a near full ride that required only that I write the trustee a long letter of my progress and gratitude each year. The assistant of the assistant dean of studies made sure I always remembered.

Sarah Lawrence College, Bronxville, New York

Bronxville was a half-hour train ride from New York City, a home I'd decided was home long before I ever set foot in it.

But the college felt worlds away. Because I came from suburban greater Los Angeles, suburban greater New York City
felt like an insult. Imagining the melting pot of my dreams, I
did not, for instance, expect there to be more white people at
Sarah Lawrence than there were in my hometown. I was the
only Iranian there, among the whole college campus of 1,200
students. Again, there were only a couple of other Middle
Easterners.

New York's Iranian-American population was mostly
limited to the predominantly Jewish enclave of Great Neck
on Long Island, which consisted of a mere and yet relatively
impressive two thousand Iranians (20 percent of Great Neck's
population). At Sarah Lawrence, the Middle Easterners were
royalty or at least acted like it. But everybody was somebody
there. My most ordinary-seeming hallmate was Peter Gabri-
el's daughter. My name didn't stand out among the Eurydices
and Harmonys and the Afrikas. But at Sarah Lawrence I actually passed less than I did in Pasadena at first. This was not because of my complexion or my hair, but because of my *clothes*.

On the first day of college, I wore jean cutoffs and Pumas
and a wifebeater with no makeup and a ponytail—these were
my Angeleno suburban trash standbys, I suppose. I never repeated that mistake again, after seeing what my peers were
wearing, and I became a regular East Village shopper, blow-
ing sometimes the whole of my parents' hundred or so sent to
me every other month on something ostentatious and mostly
useless, like the pair of clownish platform shoes that were the
norm on Bates Hill, the "SLC runway" among the ample
foliage and Tudor cottages of the campus center at Sarah
Lawrence. My hallmates wore Prada and Gucci and gave me

their high school hand-me-downs, and more than once after a few drinks—amaretto, Chartreuse, Midori?—reminded me, in the wry double-bind delivery of true socialites, that their parents were paying for me to be at school with them. They were curious about where I was from, charmed almost to know me, but often just as I'd get started with my story, they'd cut right in and move right on. It was miserably lonely.

Meanwhile, the more academia stuffed me with theorists and writers like Derrida and Chomsky, Kierkegaard and Nietzsche, Foucault and Sartre, the more difficult I found it to talk to my family. They'd rotate the phone and I'd numbly go through the motions, praying I wouldn't explode.

"What are you learning?" my mother asked.

My mother was an accountant.

"I can't get into it. Really complicated stuff. I like it."

"Are you getting good grades?"

"We don't have grades, Mom," I reminded her with a groan.

She paused. "How have you done on your tests?"

"We don't have tests here, Mom," I snapped, starting to get nasty.

"I'll put your dad on."

He'd get on and start grilling me about the weather for a while and then also get to the irritating stuff. "So what's your major and minor?"

"We don't have those, Dad. Do you mean my concentration?"

"What?"

"Writing," I'd say, giving up. "Just don't worry about it."

"What math are you taking?" he asked.

"I'm not."

He, a math professor, would go silent. My brother, age thirteen at that time, would get on.

"Have you gone to the Empire State Building? The Statue of Liberty?"

"I live in Bronxville."

"The Bronx?"

"No, never mind," I'd grumble.

"Mom says there are drugs there. Are there drugs?"

"No," I lied. "I wouldn't know."

"Do you have friends?" he asked. I could tell my mother had planted questions in him.

"Yes. Do you, nerd?"

"What are they like?"

I didn't know who was my friend and who wasn't. I put myself through multiple makeovers—Gothish, punk-rock lite, nerdcoresque, hip hippie—but I could never manage to sink into a "scene." My solution to this unease was, just as in high school, to get away.

During my undergraduate years, I did not find a place of respite in the libraries, the bookstores, the readings, the dorms of friends and lovers, the office hours with idols, or the cubicles of internships at the greatest publications on earth. Instead New York City's nightclubs offered me a home.

I spent a lot of my time—sometimes spare, sometimes not—in clubs. Electronic music and its physical incarnation, the rave, was a tempting and great equalizer. In the subterranean universe of gut-stabbing beats, its conversation-less sea of bobbing bodies in impossibly XXXXL attire, I couldn't tell anyone apart—who was a boy or a girl—much less the misguided identifiers of otherness. I'd enter arenas, clubs, and patches of woods like a ghost in a dream, mind coated in the glitter of illegal psychoactive stimulants, and I'd exit straight to a deep viscous sleep, with no clear recollection of anything or anyone in that world of mine. In a time of *self self self*, I wonder if we clubbers kept it anonymous, impersonal, cool, blank on purpose. My uniform was a hoodie, cargo pants, a silver chain, and colorful limited-edition Nikes, preferably from Japan. I could have been a boy from the warehouse next door. Identity was irrelevant, and yet it was intentional.

But *why*? Who was I? Why? I was, in a way, taking small steps toward self-definition, ones that had nothing to do with the body I was born in, the DNA of my parents, the blood of my ancestors. I was, for instance, a smoker. I was a yoga student. I was an occasional drug dabbler—cocaine here and there and Ecstasy primarily in the city because of the constant promise of "pure MDMA." I was left politically, I guessed. I was a lover of literature. Lipstick lesbian or slutty straight—I constantly went back and forth between these, like every girl I knew—I was, in the end, neither: just a raggedy bisexual.

I was a writer, I ventured, but somehow every vision I had of that—desk, chair, pen, typewriter, books, window, dog at feet—implied that making a home was involved.

❋

I made it through one year at Sarah Lawrence, then another; after that I went abroad to Oxford, where I spent the entire time in clubs again, clubs that reminded me of New York City.

The summer before returning to New York, the summer before my senior year, I spent in a true funk and its counterpart setting for me: Los Angeles. There I was with my hood up, shielded from my native city's famed sunshine, even though I spent all my time in my little room, with the shades drawn and my phone unplugged and the door locked, among books and articles. I had it bad.

Electronic music meant less than anything now. Whereas the summer before I had spent giddily dating an ex-MTV VJ turned jungle DJ, now music without human presence seemed worthless, cheesy, and sometimes chilling. I turned to hip-hop, all words, with some beat. But that summer the words, I remember, were angry and fearful, full of warnings and paranoias.

Pop culture was reeling from the failure of Woodstock 99, an event that was defined by rape, looting, and arson. The mainstream media was in shock still over the deaths of JFK Jr. and Carolyn Bessette in a tragic plane crash. World news, meanwhile, reported India and Pakistan were at each other's throats. Everyone was talking about the impending new year and the Y2K problem. Even 9/9/99 was causing hysteria— the computers could lose their minds, as the date value was frequently used to demarcate an unknown date, not to mention 9999 was an end-of-file code in old programming languages. The very near future looked ominous, and what was worse, unknowable. So loaded, it had ended up a bit blank to all of us, and that was terrifying. There were no answers.

I hid, and I hid, and I hid.

My father knocked on the door, and I wouldn't answer. My mother knocked on the door, and I wouldn't answer. My brother slipped me notes under the door: *It's Mom's birthday*. Or *Can I borrow your boom box*? Once it was just *Snap out of it, jerkass*. I knew they missed me.

I missed *me*.

What was my problem? Everyone wanted to know. What was my problem?

I didn't discover it back then.

In retrospect, I think I had felt on the verge of discovering a me out there in the city, but I had failed somehow. All I had was a year left, senior year, to find myself, somewhere in that city.

❋

There was the old familiar relief of summer's end as I boarded that flight back to New York for my last school year—*phew, no more family till Christmas*—and after all those hours, the city's brashly visible landmarks had a certain nostalgia for me as we touched down. I took the bus from JFK to the city, where I arranged a ride up to Sarah Lawrence with my friend Natalya, a Ukrainian-born Lower East Side–raised lesbian activist who was the closest thing I had to a *real* friend as well as something of an older sister to me there. She, too, was an outsider, on scholarship as well and loaded with so many minority markers, she just laughed it—laughed everything, really—off. I met her in her family's new digs on the Upper

East Side, all part of then Mayor Rudy Giuliani's bizarrely idealistic plan to integrate the new poor with the very old rich.

"We live in a good time," Natalya's mom told me in her broken English as she gave me a tour of the many rooms of her high-ceilinged hardwood-floored apartment that looked almost bare in spite of bearing all that motley stuff that had packed their Lower East Side project to near unlivability.

I nodded numbly. They were exactly the opposite of my family: the lower class (*freakin' peasantry*, as Natalya would call them) thrust into upper-classdom. It had given them a sort of sanity and calm. I thought of my own family: old Iranian aristocrats stuffed into a tiny crummy suburban apartment, with nothing to show of their pedigree but the insanity of those who once had everything and were forced to abandon it all, almost overnight.

Natalya and I made our way to our college campus mostly in silence, mine largely ruling over hers in a way that made her give up conversation instantly, eyeing me nervously the whole ride instead. On the Metro-North train, I watched Midtown become Harlem become the Bronx become Westchester, and I paid for our short cab ride to campus. My new dorm room was tiny and on the first floor, so I could watch everyone come and go. And there they were: the hippies, the punk rockers, the hip-hoppers, the ravers, the Goths, the mods, the butches, the femmes, the freaks. Not much had changed.

But I had changed, although I didn't realize it yet.

In the next month, as 9/9/99 came and went with no disturbances, I carried on, arguing with typical SLC fervor in my Postmodern Lit class, charging cartons of cigarettes to my parents' bookstore account, shuttling back and forth to the city for my internship at *Spin* magazine. I carried on and on. I handed out all my electronic CDs and vinyl to the late adopter raver wannabes on my floor, and I began adding to my old hip-hop collection. Gang Starr and Tupac and old N.W.A. were blasting from my dorm. Not an eyebrow raised my way.

I got braided extensions down to my ass and wore hoop earrings, a new sort of baggy pants, and too much makeup. I told my boss at *Spin* in horrific fake hip-hop twang that I wanted to work at their sister magazine *Vibe*. I went to Universal Zulu Nation meetings, where I asked too many questions, and then I went straight to clubs that played hip-hop. At one point, a black DJ I was hanging out with tugged at my braids and asked me if I was biracial—*half black*, he even clarified—and I said, with little hesitation, *yes*. And then I went home and cried all night—I had collapsed into a meaningless lie. Although that was before I understood that my father's side had Afro-Iranian roots and there were more truths there than I had access to uncover. Still, I never returned his phone calls.

This final expression of my cultural confusion was the perfect explosion. My numbness and unknowing grabbed at whatever it could latch on to. The lack of definition led to spontaneous definition, a stray, irresponsible, chaotic, hurtful lie. A shoplifted attempt at ownership. The aughts taught me, just a typical bicoastal, bicultural *other*, real lessons.

The first lesson: I could be myself, and that self honestly, truly, terribly did exist.

It didn't take the entirety of the aughts—just two years

after that SLC homecoming, long after we all survived Y2K just fine. I gave up my first apartment in New York, a ramshackle Park Slope garden apartment with clashing roommates, and transitioned to my boyfriend's glossy studio, twenty-five floors up, in a then-rare East Village high-rise, with a view of the entirety of lower Manhattan and beyond. The first tear appeared in the fabric then, leaving me to hope only that I wouldn't live long enough to see more.

I woke up fast, first thing on a bright sunny Tuesday morning in 2001. I was twenty-three and still in limbo. In spite of my internships and freelance work here and there and interviews galore, I was hopelessly unemployed and had been for almost a year then. But I woke up, saw it all, and never turned back. It took a world to crumble around me to learn who I was.

I was a New Yorker.

An Iranian in Mississippi

In the spring of 2000, I was lost. Mere months from college graduation, I could no longer hold it together to be the student I had been for nearly four years. The drinking, smoking, unstable flings, and weird friends (at one point a stripper was living with me, sleeping in my twin bed) made it so I could no longer concentrate. All my classes—the usual fiction workshop, lit class, and philosophy class; all I ever took at Sarah Lawrence, where you could take anything you wanted with no grades and no exams and still be encouraged to complain—seemed a burden. I added one independent study with my American Studies professor that was meant to be journalistic somehow. I was supposed to be giving it direction, and I had none.

Professor Lyde Sizer and I would stare at each other during tense office hours, every second feeling like an hour.

"Your skin is gray," she once said to me.

I had nothing to say, because I no longer looked in mirrors, but I trusted her.

"Are you depressed?" she asked. "When was the last time you were excited? What excited you?"

I was sick of my friends, going out, substances, so my mind went to books. "I used to read a lot," I finally said.

"Go on."

"I loved it."

Professor Sizer smiled at me, "Now you sound more like yourself. Keep going."

She had never known what *I* was like, so I didn't believe her, but I went on because there was nothing else to do.

In all my years at college, this was the first time I had spoken of William Faulkner, my first literary love. I had just come back from a year abroad at Oxford because that was where I thought I could study the Western canon as myself. Identity politics were at a fever pitch, and I was tired of living in so many margins: I was brown, bisexual, from a Muslim background, of the dreaded Middle East, of the even more reviled Iran, always poor from parents who were originally not poor and then had become very poor. I was sick of the fringes. At Oxford, I could get the most conventional Western education possible: I read the classics like Dante, Shakespeare, the Old and New Testaments. But American literature didn't hit the surface with my professors. Faulkner didn't come up once.

"What was it about him?" Professor Sizer asked.

How do you explain to anyone why you, as a fifteen-year-old suburban Pasadena, California, teenager, latched on to Faulkner? How do you explain that when your best friend had picked up the Vintage paperback of *The Sound and the Fury*, the one with the pink and blue sunset, and recommended it to you, you had just rolled your eyes? That you had told your English teacher you wanted to write your author report for honors English on Faulkner, and he disapproved, knowing you'd need a whole year to read into his books.

There was no explaining how. The text just moved me. His books were hard to understand, and I developed a strategy. *You just keep going, you plow through it*, I told my best friend, who would look over my shoulder after school, perplexed by the gift she had handed down. *You just keep going, you plow through it*, I would tell my Columbia MFA students in a seminar twenty years later.

"But what was it about him?" I thought maybe it was the language—the maximal stream of consciousness somehow mirrored my own psyche, the lush style and winding rhythms of Southern writing somehow reflecting the lattice and arabesques of my own first language, Farsi. (A decade later my comp-lit-studying brother told me that Middle Easterners have a special affinity for Faulkner.) Perhaps there was something of the story of the South too: its rise and fall, the Reconstruction era and beyond, the blood in the soil, the civilization on a pedestal and then questioned and then lost.

But I wasn't thinking about all that then—I was thinking about making some kind of an escape for myself. I told her all

I did know, and then I said, "I don't know why he spoke to me, but maybe I could find out," and right then I had an idea.

I could go to Oxford, Mississippi, where Faulkner lived, couldn't I? I could find out if I belonged where Faulkner had belonged.

I imagined Professor Sizer looking at me mockingly, so when I got the courage to meet her eyes, I was surprised. She looked earnest, nodding her head. "I think that's the best idea you've had for me ever," she said.

And so for my spring break of senior year, just months before I would begin my life as a college graduate in New York City, I set off to the Deep South to find something, anything, of a self I didn't quite know I'd lost.

❋

It was the first time I took an airplane ride that didn't follow a route determined by my parents, and not between LAX and JFK. I was flying to Memphis, Tennessee, which I had discovered was the only way to get to Oxford, Mississippi. Then I would ride a Greyhound Bus to Oxford. I learned this from phone calls to the Faulkner estate and museum, where a curator named Bill Griffith had offered to meet me and put me in touch with Southern Studies students at the University of Mississippi in Oxford.

I had no idea what I was doing, but I told myself I had no other choice. Youth told me—falsely, of course—that I'd never have an adventure like this again, and that I had to see more of the South while I was down there, and that perhaps a day or two in Memphis was the right thing. I booked two nights at a chain motel near Graceland. Elvis was an icon I had largely ignored, but I thought lodging nearby would be a good idea: nice area, full of tourists, no big deal for a young woman like me who had seen it all in New York.

Upon arrival, I realized Graceland was not in the best part of town—I didn't know what the best was, but it couldn't have been what I arrived into. I walked to a gas station to get some water bottles and found there was no sidewalk on the main road. I walked carefully alongside the road, the lone pedestrian, as cars honked and young guys hooted at me from their windows. At first I imagined I was in my native Los Angeles, where walking in the streets was rare, but there was something different in the air here. I wasn't sure if it was my cutoff jean shorts that were somehow inappropriate or that somehow these guys could tell I was *different*. By the time I got back to the motel room, my heart was racing. What had I done? Where was I? Who was I?

My dark, dusty motel room offered little consolation. I remember sitting for hours alone on the creaking twin bed, trying to cancel out the smells of conflicting body odors—not mine!—by eating soy jerky I'd brought from New York. I was a vegetarian and had no idea what was in store for me foodwise. I sat and ate, my mind mostly blank except for its being paralyzed with fear.

By morning, I submitted to my setting and took the Graceland tour and then even took a tour of downtown Memphis. Graceland was cramped, full of kitsch, a place of stale Elvis jokes, sad and camp. It seemed equally disappointing to everyone on the tour with me. And all I remember now of

Memphis is the Peabody, a big gilded grand hotel where the claim to fame was a daily duck processional through the lobby. This was less disappointing, but it didn't mean much to me.

All around Memphis, a bleak sprawl reminded me of Los Angeles; there was a quiet tension that I recognized from the days following the L.A. riots. I did not belong in the discussion here. Had I come all this way to not belong all over again? To compare this to what I knew and to come up short, as all who do not belong do? Why was I here again? I wondered.

I remember walking again along that sidewalk-less highway, this time to buy cigarettes—much cheaper than they were in New York—and ordering my first biscuits and molasses at a lonely diner. Was this the real world? Before I could even attempt to answer those questions, the next morning—drizzly and gray—I was on a Greyhound bus, arriving in no time at all in Oxford, Mississippi.

❋

Bill Griffith, a tall man with curly brown hair and kind brown eyes—the sort of guy who had the look of universal trustworthiness—picked me up at the bus station and drove me to Faulkner's once home, Rowan Oak, a literary landmark.

It was a house both tall and slight, awkward and grand, a rigid white columned mansion in the woods, the smallest example of what I didn't know then was called Greek Revival architecture. A row of cedar trees lined the driveway. It was an 1840s structure bought by Faulkner in the 1930s and renovated extensively. Faulkner gave it the name Rowan Oak—after a tree of Scottish legend that is supposed to signify security—and this was the location where his mythical Yoknapatawpha County came to life, the bulk of his books having been written here, the kitchen being where he got the call concerning his Nobel Prize. He lived here until 1962, and then it was the Faulkner home until 1972, when his daughter, Jill—who was born in the house—sold it to the University of Mississippi.

We stood in the main lobby, me nibbling on granola bars I'd packed from New York. Bill was an affable guy, not as Southern as I'd imagined, excited to talk about New York. He'd arranged one night in the alumni house for me, and for the rest of the week, I was to stay with Robin Morris, a Southern Studies student I'd managed to reach over email.

I had spoken to Bill once over the phone and he'd mentioned getting in touch with Jimmy, apparently Faulkner's oldest living relative, a seventy-seven-year-old nephew who was known to be identical to Faulkner.

"He likes to go on about it all," Bill said with a mischievous grin to me, just moments before dialing Jimmy.

After they spoke a few words on the phone, it turned out he'd be coming to see us.

"Oh wow," I cried both in excitement and in anguish, digging into my purse for spare batteries and tape for my tape recorder, nervous I'd not get my story.

"It's not that unusual," Bill assured me, more consolation than slight.

He filled me in about Jimmy, who was one of the two sons of William's brother, John, (The other, nicknamed Chooky, was around but wasn't as *social,* as Bill euphemistically put it.) Jimmy was a World War II Marine fighter pilot, and he had also fought in the Korean War. He had an engineering degree and had owned a construction company; he'd been retired for over fifteen years. Apparently "Brother Will" (the only way he referred to William Faulkner) had called him "the only person who likes me for who I am." For all these reasons, he had become the primary Faulkner family spokesman and informal historian.

Soon enough he made it there, a slight, white-haired old man, with eyebrows and a mustache that refused to blanch quite that far, an aristocratic nose, and piercing blue eyes—indeed, a carbon copy of any Faulkner image I'd ever seen.

He asked my name and asked it again.

"Pia?" he said. "I can't hear well. Pia, is that it?"

Bill tried to correct, but I jumped in. "Pia is great."

No one had called me Pia before, but for whatever reason I thought it might be the best way to go. I was nervous, and the politics of my Iranian name was the last thing I needed to throw into the mix. I was tiptoeing, still a few days from realizing that in this region there was only black and white, and this was going to be the first place in my life that I would pass as 100 percent white.

Bill walked us through the house, but I was mesmerized by Jimmy—*I was in contact with a living, breathing Faulkner.*

By the time we finished, he turned to me and wondered what time I wanted to get up tomorrow.

I had no idea what he meant and must have looked confused.

"Well, don't you want to see some things?" he said.

"You don't want to miss this," Bill whispered in my ear, perhaps worried I was hesitating.

"I'm in," I remember saying, a sentence I would say again and again in my life to subjects whenever there was a fork in the road. "I'm in for whatever."

I remember that night feeling a little less lost, thinking I had a piece of myself I had never found in college: *I was a person who could be in for things.* I could do this, and probably could do it again and again.

❊

The Center for the Study of Southern Culture at the University of Mississippi—"Ole Miss," as I was slowly though uneasily getting used to saying—was over two decades old, a place "to investigate, document, interpret, and teach about the American South through academic inquiry and publications, documentary studies of film, photography, and oral history, and public outreach programs." It was a program in a public coed research university, Mississippi's largest university, which had well over twenty thousand students attending. I meanwhile was coming without a major—all Sarah Lawrence students graduated with a generic liberal arts diploma. Even academically, I was from a different planet.

Robin, the Southern Studies student I'd connected with, decided I could stay at her apartment as long as I wanted. She was an always smiling, always helpful, bottle-blond nerd—all novel to me. I experienced many firsts with her: She was the first stranger I ever sent an email to (since 1994, I'd been online in chat rooms, but I'd never actually emailed a stranger). The first Southern woman I'd befriended. The first graduate student I had ever met. And she had the first foldout couch I'd ever slept on.

Robin introduced me to some of her friends, and that meant going to bars and restaurants around the main square. It was with her that I tried grits and hush puppies for the first time, foods that would come to be favorites of mine. Even the air was something I was to notice—they told me to take it in, that mix of magnolia blooms and bourbon, could I smell it? I closed my eyes and concentrated and let that particular delicate sweetness rush over me, and realized that I could. They laughed knowingly and I came to understand it was a game for them at first—*let's see what the New York girl can take*—but even I was surprised at how at home I felt with it all.

It was also the first time I was *a New York girl*. In New York I was an L.A. girl. In L.A., an Iranian girl. But here there was no other interpretation. "You are so New York," one of Robin's friends said, though I couldn't bring myself to get her to elaborate. I took it as a compliment.

One place they seemed determined to take me was Graceland Too. At first I thought this was because I told them I'd been to Graceland—perhaps they thought I was an Elvis fanatic—but then it became clear to me: it was a major destination. Thirty miles north of Oxford, in Holly Springs, there was a private home that was an informal Elvis museum, a sort of shrine to Elvis by an eccentric guy named Paul MacLeod who stayed up twenty-four hours a day they said to give these "tours."

It was also something students in town did after drinking. That evening at a local bar, beers would appear in front of me, with someone, usually Robin's friend Josh, shaking his head and saying, "Trust me, you're gonna need it."

We made it there well into the early hours of the morning. Indeed, the rumors of the owner having altered his face surgically to resemble Elvis seemed true—at least, an Elvis-looking man greeted us at the door of this ramshackle home, collected five dollars from each of us, and then spent what felt like many, many hours talking at us nonstop as he took us from room to room filled floor to ceiling with Elvis memorabilia, from stamps to books to albums to dolls to seemingly anything imaginable that was Elvis-themed. I remember at one point it felt as though we'd never get out. (MacLeod's story had a strange end. In July 2014, he was found dead on the Graceland Too porch, two days after fatally shooting a visitor who appeared to be a burglar.)

On the car ride back, I was in the backseat with Josh, the Alabama grad student who seemed impossibly foreign to me. I rested my head on his shoulder as I fell asleep. "Welcome to the South," I remember him saying. I must have snapped into consciousness and replied something, because I remember his telling me, "And your adventure is just about to begin."

❊

I came to the adventure of William Faulkner, but soon it was clear to me that Jimmy Faulkner was the real adventure. For the next ten days, this man became a daily part of my life.

"Good morning, Pia," he'd say at seven a.m., which felt late to him because he always rose at five. *Farmer's hours*, Bill explained to me, even though Jimmy was not a farmer and never had been.

To him, I became an Italian New York girl named Pia who had a fancy job in publishing—he kept forgetting I was a student and instead focused on my magazine internship. As much as I'd tell him I was an intern and had no power, he'd insist it was an important job. At times I worried that he thought I was a key to his getting a potential book by John Faulkner published; I started to think that was why he was interested in driving me for hours all around the county, showing me "secret Faulkner spots," but Bill told me Jimmy would occasionally take a liking to a visitor and give them the extended tour. I was relieved.

We went to all sorts of places. One afternoon he drove us to the banks of the Tallahatchie River. Some of his friends were there, and they looked like they were pacing looking for something. "Confederate gold," Jimmy explained, and soon I saw several of them had metal detectors. "They say there's something," Jimmy went on halfheartedly, like someone who maybe knew better or maybe not.

Another day we were in the cemetery, where he told me stories about obscure relatives. In his home, he showed me Confederate currency in a sock drawer and then made me an afternoon omelet. We paused at a truck stop diner—a thing in the South, I realized!—where I listened to his endless stories while discovering the joys of collards and candied yams—my new favorite side dishes.

Several times we went by Square Books in the center of town, where Jimmy was treated as a celebrity, before the giant Faulkner displays. He'd show me all the fruits of the various annual Faulkner conferences and all his talks, with the pride of a man who late in life had become a scholar. Faulkner was still more popular than the other big writer in town, Jimmy seemed to proudly grumble, referring to John Grisham, whose massive compound in the hills seemed to look down on the city.

Another time he said he wanted to take me to a juke joint. I had no idea what that was and played along. I remember feeling slightly uneasy after we pulled up to what looked like a tin shack off the side of a very green highway, with a bunch of cars crowding a dirt path. "Here we are," Jimmy said, smiling mischievously. It turned out that this was Chulahoma, "Junior's Place," built by the great Mississippi hill country blues legend Junior Kimbrough and now run by two of his sons (he was rumored to have had thirty-six children) since his death a couple of years earlier. I was familiar with Junior because Moby had recently released his album *Play*, and that had got me interested in the blues musicians on Oxford's Fat Possum Records—who had produced Kimbrough in his final years. I later learned that juke joints were both lovely and sad places—created out of necessity, the refuge of plantation workers and sharecroppers after the Emancipation Proclamation, since there were still no public spaces that allowed black people to mix with whites. That sadness followed it to the end: just a few months after I visited it, this historic juke joint burned down.

My best memory of all from those ten days is an early

one. In one of my first nights spending time with him, Jimmy invited me to a family gathering at his favorite place, Taylor Grocery. This was a strange sort of run-down mom-and-pop restaurant that had an amazing reputation in town, packed with families and music playing—a cozy, cramped dining establishment full of red-checked tablecloths. Jimmy didn't ask what anyone wanted, and when the waitress came over, he ordered for all of us. I was too busy taking in the atmosphere to even notice, and soon sweet tea appeared before me and eventually a big plate of . . . fried catfish.

As I mentioned, I was a vegetarian, a strict one for eight years, and I had snacks on me at all times for emergencies like this. I knew there was no way I could eat that fish and yet there was no way I could say no. I tried for a second to reach into my purse for a bag of nuts and explain to Jimmy, but he, hard of hearing, was yelling louder than ever in that busy dining room, telling me not to be afraid, I'd love it— he knew it was my first catfish (though we'd never discussed vegetarianism). I realized I had no choice. Gingerly I cut into it and slathered it in sauce and took a bite, cringing. And then another and another. I didn't pause to think about the taste. Lost in that evening of music and laughter and conversation, I felt a part of Jimmy's world.

I assumed I'd spend the night ill, but instead when I got back to Robin's, I lay in bed unable to sleep. I was full of energy, an energy unlike any I'd experienced in ages. This was the start of my pescatarianism, which lead to omnivorism. At least I could say a Faulkner did it to me.

Here was another piece of me. I was a person who could overstep my own beliefs, who could become someone else.

Pia, Italian, New York Girl, fish-eater—none of those things held me back. They reminded me that I, at twenty-two, could perhaps be anyone I wanted, and perhaps even one day in the ways that I wanted.

❋

Jimmy and I would sometimes spend eight-hour days together with only bits of silence here and there. Often I was asking questions and recording him, but other times we were just two friends hanging out, with no conversational agenda. One time he asked me about my family. I almost got into our years as immigrants, and how I wished I could one day go back to Iran, when he cut in: "Do they live in Italy still?" I shook my head. "No, they're in California." He looked sad for a second, as if he knew. But instead he said, "This land is all I've ever known and will know."

Eventually it was time to go home, back to college, where my time was dwindling. I had just a few weeks to go. Jimmy and Robin and pretty much everyone asked me what I'd do next and if I'd be back. I said I obviously would, but I didn't know if that was true. Travel was then a confusing concept— all I knew was that I was moving to Brooklyn after graduation and there was no telling what would come of that. I felt like I was a real journalist on that trip, but I didn't know if I could be one in New York, or become the self I had gotten to be in Mississippi for a brief period.

Jimmy insisted on driving me to the airport in Memphis. He maintained that he didn't mind the long trek and assured me that once I was gone, his days would feel empty. He insisted on carrying my bags, though I walked him back to his car. There he gave me a long hug and leaned in to a kiss, which missed my cheek and reached my lips. I laughed shyly, then realized it wasn't a complete accident: "I'm telling you, Pia, if you were older, and I was younger . . ." He left it at that, and we left it at that. It was a sentiment he returned to again in one of the many letters he wrote me after I moved to New York, long letters in his beautiful handwriting, detailing his days, and only once in a while hoping that perhaps one day I could help to get John Faulkner's work published.

For a while I wrote him back, but eventually either he or I stopped responding, and the experience left my mind, as I was busy dealing with finding some sort of footing as an adult.

Years went by, and then one day I found his letters again and thought I'd look him up. What I found was sad, though not surprising: He had died at seventy-nine, two years after my visit. It seemed hard to imagine, given his vitality. I felt crushed, remembering his letters. I also felt lucky.

In 2008, my then boyfriend and I drove cross-country and stopped in Oxford, Mississippi, for a couple of nights. I remembered more than I thought I would even after eight years. "Welcome to Lafayette County!" I announced, as if I were a native. A couple of months before, the first presidential election debate of 2008 had taken place there, and that was the only context my boyfriend had. He was not a literary person, so I broke down for him my early love of Faulkner, and the Brother Will I discovered through Jimmy Faulkner, as we pulled up to the twin cedars of Rowan Oak.

"It's seems like you've lived here for ages," he said. "Like you've come home."

There was a lot he did not understand when I tried to tell him. I had been Italian? I had broken my vegetarianism? (He was vegan.) I had just stayed with students? This had all meant the world to me?

I didn't feel like explaining.

Hand in hand, we walked into Rowan Oak; I was shaking with so many emotions. Bill happened not to be there when we dropped by, but he was still the curator, an assistant assured us. This time I had a camera and took photos; the wallpaper on my computer is Faulkner's office wallpaper, captured on my camera from that trip. My boyfriend walked with me through it all, patiently absorbing my enthusiasm.

And that was fine. We took a walk in the woods, and I told him if he closed his eyes and breathed deeply, he could smell the mix of magnolia blooms and bourbon, but he couldn't. And there was something I loved about that.

"Not bad." Professor Sizer had grinned, a rare expression of approval from her, as I handed her the thirty pages of my final assignment.

I didn't get it back until years later, when I returned to Sarah Lawrence to give a reading as a published author. Professor Sizer had wanted to give my introduction, and she concluded her remarks with "I have something for you," then handed me my paper in front of a large audience. I had gotten an A−, and light pencil marks wound all the way through it. I thanked her and thanked her in my head all through the reading, but also thanked everyone I had encountered on that trip, especially Jimmy.

I also thanked that gray-skinned, frazzled, listless twenty-two-year-old who lived with being so lost that there was no choice but to allow herself, on a most unlikely adventure, to be found again.

The King of Tehrangeles

Once upon a time—okay, 2005—I was a Rodeo Drive shop-girl. I was a college graduate, even the holder of a master's, and fairly prideless, having been through many jobs, from nanny work in New York to bistro bussing in Baltimore. I moved back home to Pasadena, California, to save money while I worked on a novel that I felt I would never finish.

I had worked in sales many times by then, but nowhere of this sort—half the boutique's handbags, made of the skins of species that seemed like they ought to be endangered, cost well over the highest annual income I had made at that point. I was overdressed in the required all black, sulking, daydream-ing, lingering at the window with a dust rag, counting all the passersby luckier than I, waiting for the sun to go down, when I could lock up and forget the non-events of the day.

During the rare occasion when a customer came in—I was the sole shopgirl at a store that averaged three to six people per day—I'd quickly tell them to come back next week when we'd have a sale—which we never had—because I was too anxious to ring up something in the five figures.

Once in a while I amused myself by taking ambitious breaks, usually to the less desirable end of Rodeo, the slums of Jamba Juice, Sprinkles Cupcakes, and Le Pain Quotidien. Other times I'd only make it to look into the shop window across the street, to that all-yellow store with the matching yellow luxury vehicle propped outside. I wasn't permitted to enter.

First, the store was by appointment only, as the sign on the door insisted. Second, it was the House of Bijan—the flagship store of Iranian-American icon Bijan, designer of jewelry, fragrances, and luxury menswear, renowned as the man behind the most expensive store in the world, the pride and joy of my fellow Iranians for its exclusivity. I couldn't go in precisely because of my Iranianness. I was the wrong kind, the anomaly of anomalies in L.A.: the poor Iranian, that incomprehensible being who received either the cold disregard or the flushed pity of rich Iranian ladies who'd nervously fondle my clutches and totes, always mortified at the disgrace of my very existence. *Persian girl, how did this happen to you?* a heavily bejeweled elderly Iranian woman, turning up what must have been her third or fourth nose, once said to me as she spotted me sweeping outside the store.

I was one of many Iranians fascinated by the mess of yellow in and out of the palazzo-inspired $122 million, thirty-five-year-old 90210 landmark. Everything was gilded: the obscenely luminous marble floors, the imperious flower arrangements, the Disney-princess sweeping staircase, the mammoth chandelier made of his signature perfume bottles, and, of course, the signature yellow Ferrari or Bugatti or Rolls outside, giving you the sense that Bijan *lived* there. The other notable element inside was the utter emptiness (I would sometimes still look in the window), apparently not a sign of bad business, but evidence that almost no one could afford the place—the way Bijan liked it. "I am not a mass designer," he told the *Los Angeles Times* in 2003. "What was important to me was not to have two million clients, like Versace, but to have twenty thousand clients." And so it followed that on any given day, you'd see a flock of my people huddling with cameras outside the store. Nobody was allowed in, but it didn't matter. It wasn't what was inside that was the point; it was about the gilded surface—again, just as Bijan would have liked it.

Bijan died April 16, 2011, at Cedars-Sinai Medical Center in Los Angeles after suffering a stroke at age seventy-one, though he had insisted that year that he was sixty-seven. Bijan had hit the mark of twenty thousand clients times two, apparently. His yearly revenue was in the billions, he reported. He was known for dressing celebrities like Tom Cruise and Anthony Hopkins, as well as thirty-six different presidents all over the world. "My favorite are the Americans," he coos on his website video. Apparently even President Obama was a Bijan man. Bijan luxury items range from $1,000 suits to $120,000 chinchilla bedspreads. In a video on his website, he gushes, "I happen to be the most expensive clothing designer for the world!" And then he adds, "And I'm sorry for that," sounding anything but sorry.

This is how you imagine the King of Tehrangeles would carry himself. But even while he was perched on the pinnacle of rampant excess and unfathomable wealth and gold-plated garishness, all the stuff of a Liberace fever dream that were the emblems of Iranian exile style in the Southern California hub, it seemed sometimes as if Bijan was a little bit in on the joke.

Bijan's sense of humor seemed evident in that gaping half smirk, half guffaw he'd brandish on his billboards, like a smile was the essential accessory. His was often featured in his own ad campaigns, especially the ones that strove for controversy with their risqué humor. For example, in 1995, he featured Bo Derek—in his beloved Bo-braids phase (according to *The New York Times*, he once had "$20 million worth of diamonds braided into Ms. Derek's hair for a perfume campaign")—opening up her trench coat against the camera, presumably exposing her infamous body to a comically aghast Bijan and his hand-over-eyes-posing four-year-old son. Then five years later, inspired by Botero paintings, he used a nude plus-size model Bella as his mock lover in a campaign that caused many magazines to initially refuse to run it until *Talk* magazine caved, allegedly because of Tina Brown's friendship with Bijan. Bijan was also known for the ad that hit closer to his old home: a veiled Muslim beauty with the caption: "Jammal, you might as well know the truth. . . . I'm in love with Bijan." His ads were always included in nineties "shockvertising" studies, but Bijan was not obsessed with the hip or edgy.

He loved the larger than life, iconhood. His muses were huge, from Bella to Michael Jordan, whose cologne he put his name on when the two partnered for the successful venture.

Blame this on his sense of humor, too: in 1982, he created a gold designer gun. He told *Time*: "I wanted to make something so American. I wanted to design a gun that people who hate guns would want to have and touch and play with because it's so pretty." The $10,000 limited edition .38-caliber Colt revolver was made of fifty-six grams of twenty-four-karat gold and sold in a mink pouch with a Baccarat crystal case embossed with the customer's name.

Iranians have wanted to love him, but it wasn't always easy. My family, distanced at a half hour and many bank account zeros from Tehrangeles, had mixed emotions about Bijan. When we'd be out in Westwood for a Saturday kebab lunch, my dad would always excitedly point out his billboards and then immediately tag on, "Big Bear, so *loose!*" (A less literal translation: "Grown-ass man, so." *Loose* is impossible to translate accurately, but it's a cross between silly, gross, embarrassing, cloying, hideous, and precious.) When his women's fragrance DNA came out in 1993, at a typical mall outing, I observed my mother's reaction to the eau de parfum spray scent. It was like watching a cycle of daylight and darkness. She'd be wide-eyed and smiling pre-sniff, fight to retain the brightness post-sniff, become half disappointed, and grow dark at a final glance at the price tag.

And yet who can deny some joy for my brethren who, in the eighties and nineties, achieved fame without being a terrorist? Bijan beat Americans at their own game—he saw the punch line and made it his and won over potential naysayers with his greatest weapon: the blinding light of flamboyance and ostentation. He embodied American overindulgence to the maximum. He was the creator of Tehrangeles flash and trash, an exuberant succumbing to American capitalism combined with an old-country-gentry national-pride-on-steroids complex. Bijan was monarchy in everlasting exile, the émigré owning his abroad. You needed gold, marble, fountains, and columns to carry that off; you needed the brazen optimism of yellow, a shade not unlike the yellow gold of the Iranian lion, the centerpiece of the pre-revolutionary Iranian flag.

Is this the beginning of the end of the Tehrangeleno golden period? Crossover Iranians, after all, have taken steps off the pedestal. Cameron Alborzian, an early nineties supermodel (most famous as Madonna's plaything in the "Express Yourself" video), is now a yoga teacher. Googoosh, Iran's disco-era Madonna, had a cosmetics line and for a limited time was depressingly advertising free hats with any purchase. There was even a (now shuttered) website devoted to showcasing the darkest side of Iranian-American assimilation: the monstrous McMansions that have multiplied over the decades in Tehrangeles: uglypersianhouses.com.

It's hard not to take Bijan's passing in 2011 as the end of an era. He was the last of a sort of unapologetic breed of obscenely affluent out-of-touch Iranians. One can imagine Bijan is most himself in yellow and gold eternally up above—in the campy heaven of harps and cherubs, the afterlife with angels of the Victoria's Secret kind frolicking on clouds, the razzle-dazzle paradise.

✳

Years after my shopgirl stint, over the shit jobs and past my first novel's publication, I drove cross-country with my then boyfriend. Somewhere in gray rural Tennessee, I saw a giant truck with a familiar image on it: elegant scrawl and a doughnut-shaped glass bottle. It was a Bijan ad.

I got very, very excited.

Who is Bijan? my boyfriend asked as I took photos.

A designer, I told him. *The Iranian-American designer.*

You like his stuff? he asked.

I hate it! I said and snapped some more.

For a moment, I was a shopgirl again, staring at the signature that was the symbol of Bijan as it sped off in front of us, always steps ahead in some race I never quite understood, and yet somehow, against all odds, suited for the fabric of even the worst of this country.

Blond Girls

As long as I can remember, I've had a sick fascination with American blonds. Old movie classics were how this Iranian-American immigrant learned English—my early diary entries are full of mid-Atlantic-accented leading-lady coos like "Ain't life grand!" and "Golly!" Between the AMC channel and the wonderful local indie video store, my psyche was firmly molded by eras past. I'd take Marilyn Monroe, Jayne Mansfield, Jean Harlow, and Betty Grable over sitcom ingenues and *Tiger Beat* fare any day. But when I'd pose with a black crayon dangling from my lips, draped in my aunt's furs, tangled in costume jewelry, I knew I was playing someone I was not.

I was no blond.

By my teenage years, I'd given up starlet drag. In the nineties, I lusted after a different type of iconic blond—the Kurt and Courtney white-hot grunge blond; Kat Bjelland's Babes in Toyland wackadoodle baby-doll blond; Kim Gordon's effortless X-Girl introvert blond—but none of these was quite *me*, either. The first feminine icon I aspired to realistically look like was Dil of *The Crying Game*, a wiry, scrawny, dark-haired It Girl who—spoiler—was trans. PJ Harvey and Lisa Bonet were my only brunette iconoclast icons of sexiness. With my mustache, unruly eyebrows, and beanpole physique, I tried to convince myself I was keeping it real. I was the smarty-pants, the outcast, the weirdo, the rebel. I never dared to touch blond's pageant-queen mainstream.

The other issue was my mother. To this day I've seen my mother's natural hair color only in old photos; apparently it was once jet-black like mine. I've also rarely seen my mother without makeup, perhaps only when I've glimpsed her fresh out of a shower. My mother is the kind of woman who wears lipstick to the pool, who suffocated the one yoga class I took her to in Chanel No. 5, who once told me she'd commit suicide when her looks went. In the eighties, she'd L'Oréal the full spectrum of red and yellow, from copper to bronze to gold to platinum and back again, the long, feathered, perfect hair that she spent hours on daily. Her appearance was her main object, the one link and key to acceptance that she carried from Iran to the United States. Never mind that she'd dropped several tiers of social class in the transition. She could make stonewashed imitation Guess jeans from JCPenney look just as elegant as the YSL suits of her Tehran twenties, procured during family shopping trips to Italy and France. Who was I to compete with that? She'd chase me around the house brandishing lipstick and tweezers, and threaten my hair with goo, all while remaining a beauty mystery to me: the foxy lady all my scrappy guy friends would turn into perfect princes around, a paragon of soap-star impeccability.

Of course, it now makes sense to me why her hair was always blondish—in Los Angeles, not only did the blond reign supreme, but also the Iranian-Americans of Tehrangeles (portmanteau for the Westside neighborhoods that are filled with Iranians) kept to blond bombshelling almost as a rule. Designer black power suits and leather little somethings, gold chains and giant rocks, stilettos and red lipstick, or perhaps something frosted—but always topped off by big hair, often a very expensive shade of flaxen. Like nose jobs, hair that was at the very least heavily highlighted was a thing. Maybe it was *truly* an Iranian fascination—I recall my father once trying to justify, a bit grumpily, that in ancient Persia, kings would place gold dust and thread in their beards and hair, which was often already orange gold with henna.

In any case, I decided that with my jet-black hair, my curvelessness and tomboyery, I'd have to be the Other. But L.A. women were hard to escape. My father's sisters lived in gilded glamour: supermodel tall and thin, art-star social-ites who used to traverse Tehran and various European cities dressed in sixties mod, like a Peggy Moffitt/Twiggy/Penelope Tree trio. I couldn't tell you any of their natural hair colors, either—between the three, you had platinum, copper, and a Wonder Woman blue black. All of them wore minidresses and heavy cat-eye liner into old age. And, like my mother, they looked most themselves when topped with a shade of metal, generally gold.

I was interested in glamour, but I was not interested in *being* the glamour. I looked to riot grrrl punk and the hair metal of the West Coast—girls whose scruffiness made them sexy, hell-raisers who were too busy causing trouble to be beautiful, whose aura was cheap and whose allure was dirty. I wore flannels, ripped jeans, Doc Martens, slashed tights, T-shirts.

Until for a time I went blond.

❋

The truth is, I'd been blond before, kinda—it wasn't my first time being bleached, at least. As a study-abroad student at Oxford, I let the small salon in the center of town turn me "cyberpunk China doll," as they called it, which meant my hair was lightened so that red streaks could show. It's just hair, I mused, a bit unsure. Six years later, at the salon Art + Science in Chicago, they shaved half my head, bobbed the other half, and applied unnatural hues in variegated bleached streaks. Just hair—I waved it off. And in 2007, just before my first novel was published, out of the anxiety and frustration of waiting, I walked into New York City's Mudhoney Salon on a whim and said I wanted black and white skunk stripes, à la Cruella de Vil.

Never ever did I want to be a full-on bottle blond. But it just so happens that I was, and am, working on a third novel that I'm calling *Tehrangeles,* largely about the fake-blond

94

Iranian-American hellions of L.A.'s Westside. At some point I decided much of the action would take place in malls, that the cast would be almost all women, and that the hair would be mostly blond—and, in fact, in the middle of the book there would be a lengthy meditation on blondness. I decided to method-act my writing. I thought, *What if I went there for just a month?*

It will be for a book! I told people. *For research!* I needlessly worried about all the people to tell—among them, colleagues, people I teach with. I decided to do it over winter break, when I didn't have to deal with student fascination and raised faculty eyebrows.

"It will be for a book! For research!" I explained to Aura Friedman, the one and only hairdresser I consulted, at Sally Hershberger Downtown. Aura's name was the one that came up again and again as the go-to for black-to-blond transitions, her magic having transformed unnatural blonds such as M.I.A. and Lady Gaga.

Aura ran her hands through my nearly waist-length black hair. Her first question: What was virgin, and what wasn't? I'd had some straightening treatments and mild ombré at one point, and so she recommended a dramatic chop. At this, I barely blinked. Then we discussed color. Before I could even get into what I thought would work best for me—the icy white blond with black eyebrows of *Who's That Girl*–era Madonna; the girls in all-black Alaïa with red lipstick, for example—Aura was already saying platinum. It was a thing that season, after all—just look at Rita Ora, Iggy Azalea, and Beyoncé, not to mention numerous models like Soo Joo Park and Charlotte Carey, both of whom are Aura devotees. Aura saw it as a no-brainer: "It's a strong look. The blond can be toned to fit almost every skin tone."

It took *eight and a half hours*. "I've been coloring hair for twenty years, and my experience has been that if I use a higher volume—stronger product one time and avoid a reapplication of bleach—the hair ends up lighter and is left stronger," Aura told me. "The more you reapply bleach to the hair, the weaker it will get." So we went with what she called a "standard virgin bleach application method." She applied a cream bleach, which she told me would be less abrasive than a powder, from about a quarter inch to an inch away from the scalp down to the ends.

When I emerged, I was white blond, more platinum than I ever could have imagined. The biggest shocker was that I was also still me—that I was, in fact, little like the Tehrangelina muses that I wanted to write about. Mine was the almost androgynous silver of old nineties Nadja Auermann and Kirsty Hume that Agyness Deyn and Robyn also took on a decade or so later. It was punk blond, a weird-bird blond, and therefore, a very me blond.

So me, in fact, that it was apparently still literary me: I'd channeled another muse of mine, one I'd finished writing about well over a year earlier—Zal, the protagonist of my second novel, *The Last Illusion*. He's based on a character in a Persian myth from the Shahnameh (Book of Kings), Iran's national medieval epic about a young boy banished to the wilderness for his white skin and hair, and eventually raised by a bird. In the book, my protagonist is an asexual, feral Iranian boy, born with a disease like albinism, who comes of age in 9/11-era New York City. His white skin and white-blond hair horrify his birth mother, who raises him in a cage with her dozens of pet birds. I was now my Bird Boy.

✻

Goodbye, control. With blond, you become a thing people react to—often very strongly. I had many compliments, usually from female strangers or gay males. Everyone has an opinion when you're blond; it's like having a puppy or baby on you—conversation-piece alert! My mother, ironically, wrote me every few weeks to ask when I would dye it back to its "beautiful black."

But the reactions it sparked, especially from men, told me that the boldness of the experiment caused as much fuss as the reality of the color. On Facebook I posted a photo that led several "friends" to melt down about it, accusing me of "whitewashing." I tried to tell them going blond was the most Iranian thing I'd ever done, but they didn't get it. In my Harlem neighborhood, where I lived at the time, I was also surprised. Looking "out there" in this sartorially flamboyant place usually goes rewarded, but one neighbor said he thought I'd joined the Witness Protection Program; another asked if I was okay, because "you look like you had a breakdown." Worst of all was the crazy cab ride in which my brown driver kept going on about loving white women and especially blonds and I did not realize he was trying to pick me up because I don't identify as one; he was horrified to learn I was Iranian and very much a brown woman when I finally showed him my very brunette driver's license photo.

Despite this madness, I felt a bit attached to the blond. For one thing, my intensely frizzy black hair felt healthier.

But it also, surprisingly, allowed me to be myself: the blond as a freak of nature. Blondness apparently came from a genetic mutation eleven thousand years ago in the last Ice Age, and natural blonds make up only 2 percent of the world's adult population.

Blond was oddity and exception to the rule. I felt more *interesting* as a blond than I did beautiful or sexy. It was comical to me to play it up with the all-black clothes and red lipstick I imagined living in—"the color of deception" and "love devastation" of INXS's "Suicide Blonde" was my spirit. Perhaps blond has reminded me I can't change who I am— "What you are picks its way," said Walt Whitman, a favorite line that I plucked for my senior quote in 1996.

The less I understand myself, I suspect, the more at peace I am with all my many disconnected pieces. Blond is baffling and full of contradictions, even in its most classical contemporary archetypes. Blond has always been more than just an American fascination—it is in Eastern cultures as well. The Harajuku Girls of Japan are only one of many such phenomena. But I think part of it has been its inherent surrealism. Acquired blond photographs a lot better than it feels, and the blond-maintenance regimen basically nixes bedhead and sexhead to nada (Aura's assistant Lucille told me to remind men they can't hair-pull in bed or it will all break). It's expensive, it's luxurious, it's time-consuming, it's absurd, it fools no one. The blond of feminists like my beloved writer Kathy Acker was in dialogue with that—women owning their countenance. The modern female is something outside of her realm in nature. That blond—cleverly confusing, resoundingly contrarian—was one I could get behind, feeling stronger and more confident than ever.

And when you're a child playing dress-up, part of the safety is knowing everyone can see through you, that it's a game. But somehow as grown-ups we try to conjure fantasy while desperately clinging to mass-produced reality. The great thing about extremely artificial and overtly outré personas is you go back to that childhood game and linger in the lovely oddness of transparency, a move made not by need but by want, leaving them guessing, like the mystery of a stray wink.

Portrait of the Artist as a Debut Novelist

1. Juvenilia

When I was about eleven, I wrote my first novel, an epic about "a Victorian girl." Translation: a girl from a faraway time and place, where human women wore big dresses and sat around sulking. That lifestyle was appealing to me. I was a sad kid, and the only excuse I could come up with for that was that I had been born in the wrong place at the wrong time.

My heroine happened to be eleven, with hair "the color of stallions" (translation: black) and skin of "pale wheat" (white or brown, depending on which Iranian you ask), and her name was knotty and yet "magnificent": Contessa Van Prgkhjiollzshdiyyiani.

Contessa was indoorsy and prone to fainting, her pockets weighed down with smelling salts. She was always perched gingerly on her windowsill, gazing at the outside world with mixed feelings. She eschewed friends—bores who mocked her "grand name" and her "odd, secret beauty." She had two distinguishing characteristics: (1) melancholy; (2) genius.

The manuscript exists. It is written in pencil, in cursive, on unlined white paper. I supplied the cover art, also in pencil: Contessa VP, all huge eyes, corkscrew hair, and a frown, in an elaborate hoop dress, feather pen in one gloved hand, vanity mirror in the other. I worked on it, my diaries reflect, in lieu of hanging out with friends and spending unquality time with my feuding parents. I composed on the same white desk until I was eighteen, always with the door closed.

By high school, I had stopped writing novels altogether. It would be another decade and a half before I again attempted to write a literary novel, a story that would save my life.

2. Girl Awthor

I can be fansy.
I can be tall.
I can ware hi heel shoos when I grow up.
Who am I?
Answer: A GIRL AWTHOR!
　　　　　　　—My first documented riddle, 1983

On Thursday, May 2, 2006, it's official. I am a girl author. I got a book deal.

It didn't feel real—not for the obvious reasons—but because I was sleep-deprived, destroyed by crying and crying and crying. The night before, I had seen J, a bouncy college friend, at an East Village café that neither of us could really afford. We bonded over the sheer awkwardness of being nannies with master's degrees, liberal arts graduates with some of the most expensive educations in the world. It was a nice dinner until the bill came. I remember having to leave a bad tip and saying goodbye and feeling all right, or at least a little less alone.

At some point during dinner, an old friend in Chicago texted me. Just three words: a good friend's name—misspelled—*died* and *sorry*. I called to clarify, but we had no vocabulary for this.

I have never found the right sentence for the experience of a death. "I was gutted." "I was devastated." "It killed me."

My friend was a writer and a Middle Easterner and a buddy of the most unlikely kind: a charming young ex-con with tattoos from the edges of his face to his knuckles, A had a passion for bespoke menswear, obscure wines, and even more obscure books. His wife, Z, was a barely legal sex worker and model, with sharp peasant features, those that give certain Midwestern girls an almost exotic allure, sabotaged only slightly by a mouthful of braces and street-hooker manners.

A had adopted me when I briefly lived in Chicago because I was an Iranian to his Iraqi—*old enemies*, he'd laugh. I was neck-deep in poverty—*been there, done that*, he'd say, annoyed—and a single mother to an ailing greyhound the whole neighborhood adored. A also said he had a feeling I had talent and asked to see my novel, which I never sent him, just as he never showed me the epic he wrote during his seven years in prison. Instead he took Z and me out on the town to trendy Wicker Park bistros, calling us both his wives, paying out of huge wads of cash.

He was also an unrehabilitated junkie back on a downward path that I—too wrapped up in my own dramas—could not, would not, detect.

A year and half after my greyhound and I had our last walk with A, his heart had given out at twenty-seven, maybe from speedballs or a bad batch of heroin floating around Chicago Avenue.

The night I learned of his death was the first night of pure, dead-black insomnia I have ever experienced, every hour punctuated by an overwhelmingly vibrant memory. I spent the next day in a defeated fetal squat on an oak chair in my then boyfriend's Brooklyn apartment. I hovered over my laptop for hours, bawling and trying to write a eulogy for A's tribute website, when my agent called and left a message. "I have good news," she said.

I had learned never to answer when my agent called. I would let her leave messages and throw my depressed fits in private.

Yet here it was: good news, a book deal. I freeze-framed the moments before—unusually hot spring day, another highly fraught adios with my boyfriend, my route to the R train in the Park Slope neighborhood of Brooklyn, my battered Razr telling me I've ignored a message, finally listening, and there it was.

Unicorns exist! Santa is not my parents! The world *is* just,

Contessa! I had never broken $25,000 a year, and now some validation—hell, salvation had come.

There may be a wise man somewhere who said extreme sadness and extreme happiness cannot successfully be bedfellows in a single day. But this joy—like a delicate magic shell—coated my sad, vulnerable core. A flickered out of the picture.

3. An Actual Portrait of the Young Artist

Spring 2007: A year later, I am back in New York, getting my author photo taken. I have known G, the photographer, for more than half my life. He was my high school journalism teacher in Los Angeles, and he suddenly, shortly after moving to New York, had become a great friend.

He asks to see what I've got. I open my bag and out comes dress after dress, silk, organza, crepe de chine, satin, Italian wool, all impeccably tailored and black, fit for a modern Contessa VP.

Dollar signs flap their wings through G's studio. I wave them away. *Not what it looks like*, I tell him. *Just dating a fashion designer.*

Just! G groans, rolling his eyes.

I go to the bathroom to put on makeup, a lot. The second I meet my own eyes in the mirror, the world starts to go black, and my vision is full of psychedelic pulses that the world calls stars.

I tiptoe out—on eggshells with myself—and G brings me water, snacks, his hand, a hug, the perfect questions.

I spent much of the summer and fall in the midst of serious anxiety, panic, depression, fatigue, gastritis, carpal tunnel, god knows what else—all the shattered states in the nightmare nation of chronic insomnia. I did what all people at a perceived end do before the end: I reached out, calling everyone I know, asking for help, collecting their anecdotes as cautionary tales, stories of hell, stories of hope, just stories to breathe with, to breathe through. I'd call people at the oddest hours and want words from them. *Please just stay on the phone; please tell me a story, any story.* In the worst times of my life, I could not imagine anything more powerful than my only business, my first love: stories.

4. Stars

August 2006: Panicking a bit about my finances—the final trickle of my advance doomed to coincide with my impending book tour—I apply for a job at a university in Long Island and am called back for an interview.

Just weeks before the launch of my book, on the day of the interview, I am what they call "all nerves." But in a good way. This time I have hopes. I assume the gods are on my team, since I haven't been notified otherwise.

A few bloggers have written some nice things about me. I joined a gym I can't afford, but I have joined a gym.

Iran is in the news daily. I am eating and sleeping. I have an uncanny knack for looking at clocks at exactly 9:11.

I take everything as an omen, signaling what, I don't know.

I am at a Starbucks in Park Slope, having taken on a pitifully ritualistic Frappuccino habit. I am reviewing my teaching philosophy, which sounds miserably fake, even though I love to teach.

When I stand up, there they are again, the stars. I panic. I don't have much time before I miss the train to Long Island. I am worrying about this as my vision wipes out in the aggressive sunshine beaming over the brownstone rooftops.

Fade in, and I'm slumped on the street, with a young hippie chick asking me *you okay you okay you okay?* Her eyes go back and forth from my squinting eyes to my hair, which is partially bleached white.

You passed out, she says, and points to the left. *Let's go to the hospital.*

The hospital happens to be across the street.

Not a chance, I tell her.

She protests. Eventually, I tell her the truth.

She nods sympathetically. *I don't have health insurance, either. But still.*

Somehow she wins and half carries me to the ER and then, as if to reward me, immediately disappears. I let the nurse take my temperature and my blood pressure before I run out the door. I call the university and tell them I will be late.

I fall four more times that day, but I get the job.

Back at home, I watch my unsteady hands at the keyboard hit and miss over and over as I try to keep writing. During the spring before that very bad summer, a psychic told me too much anxiety surrounding the novel would breed disaster.

5. The Very Bad Summer

September 2006: I turn the novel in. I go out to a celebration dinner with a very normal guy I have somehow started dating. I have theories about him. He is the type of guy who sees what he wants to see; he considers me an investment. He is the type of guy whose face I could never memorize, who looks familiar to everyone. I call him Snowboarding Attorney. He puts up with my constant whining and tells me I look great when I am down about seven pounds each month, with graying skin, a tipping and trembling mess. Any normal person would assume I am on drugs, and I am. At any given time, it's a combination of two to five types of pills, prescribed by people who don't know about one another, given to me by my second general practitioner, all three of my psychiatrists, the ER internist from my third summer visit to the ER, and a gastroenterologist. I am sedated and paralyzed.

I pick at a whole fish and order dessert. I make bathroom visits devoted solely to dropping benzodiazepine crumbs under my tongue, licking any residue off my finger.

The novel made it, but I didn't.

When I leave the Snowboarding Attorney that night, I applaud myself for having gotten through another date, relieved to be back at home.

I am at my parents' home, which was to be my summer editing and writing retreat. I want to die again. I look at a box of pills—I think, *This isn't me*—Ambien, Ativan, Klonopin, Celexa, Trazodone. They are like names for weapons, an army of futuristic knives, jagged and unforgiving. They will get me a few hours of sleep that will keep me alive. I am terrified. My whole life is doctors and ER rooms and shrinks, and they all shake their heads when they hear the answer to their question: "Has anything traumatic happened in the last few months?"

Yes, I tell them.

"*Traumatic* means *bad*," one doctor informs me.

They seem skeptical when I say I have a novel on the way, like a washboard-stomached woman complaining about third-trimester pains—just another part of the crazy talk, they must think. Doctors have started to turn me away—*I don't know what to tell you*, they say. All they can recommend is shrinks, and I have four. I pay for the visits without insurance, in cash or with plastic gold. I collect cards, any card.

You use the second person even now, because you have a sense of derealization—cognitive behavioral therapy lingo. Your parents say you were possessed, your boyfriend that you were haunted by ghosts. A few friends are adamant about chronic fatigue, and you have called it everything from a blip to the dead end.

"So there is nowhere to go but up, because you must know there is nothing wrong with you," Snowboarding Attorney says at the celebration dinner, then later over the phone, and in an email and over and over until finally he says he can't take it, and, besides, he still has feelings for his ex. You don't have hurt feelings. You have no feelings to hurt. You have a throbbing head, a rapidly beating heart, shaking hands, weak legs, a bad back, an acidic stomach, pinpricks and tingles and chills. Feelings are not your problem.

It is your mind you want back, that thing you write with, the thing you were born to do.

You have published a book and all you got was serious debt. It's an okay place to be. There are no surprises in debt. Everything is as solid as death. You are officially down to earth.

I move back to New York in May 2007. After months of a strange sort of rehab culled straight from my California playbook—acupuncture, Chinese herbs, beads and talismans, a revived vegetarianism—I am happy. Happy to call back all the people I have called and held hostage for advice, the doctors I harassed on weekends, my parents, who have been shocked about my depression since I arrived. Happy to call back my agent and editor and try to come up with new euphemisms for the old euphemisms for my condition. Happy to throw away the pills.

I move back to my old neighborhood in Park Slope and pray this new summer is kind. It is, mostly.

The novel is out of my hands and in purgatory before entering the world. I love that phase: the middle of the road trip, someone else driving, seeing a world outside pass by, deftly escaping resignation to thoughts, assignment to words.

6. Waiting

August 2007: My publishers tell me *The New York Times* is going to review my book, and it's tentatively slated for a date in September. I will lazily say that it is impossible to describe just how exciting that is, but I am also stressed. I have a whole month until the judgment.

Suddenly there is time. Time has a way of injecting herself into the picture when there is waiting to be done. I remember this from childhood Christmases, a strange holiday for my family to have celebrated. But there we were, my brother and I, with lists in hand and eyes glued to the small department-store plastic tree and its ribboned droppings. Time kept on and on, like cheap toilet paper.

The waiting is unbearable. I fill my days with yoga, massages, acupuncture, more therapy, and crank calls. This is the truth, sadly.

Even worse is this truth: I have a long history with this sort of thing. The first time I crank-called anyone, I was with K, my best friend growing up, in an elementary school summer somewhere, when we dialed the wrong number trying to call our friend L.

"But I am L. The *boy* L," the older gentleman on the phone insisted, chuckling. "What is your name?"

We played along, memorized the misdialed numbers and called more and more, spinning more intricate and riskier little yarns. He claimed he was a retired firefighter who liked "perky ladies," particularly our type, per our description: tall, leggy, blond *Playboy* models.

We were certain the joke was on him.

Sometime around then, I crank-called Kenya. I picked it for a report I had to write on a country for school, and thought it would be special to interview a Kenyan. The globe with its many cultures seemed surreal to me, a kid who was lonely in school and at home, never quite an American, never quite an Iranian. I started reading *National Geographic* and once, after I was crushed by a photo of a tribal chief in a Stüssy cap holding a radio, I remember praying, *Please, God, let these people still exist when I get older and go visit them!*

With the help of a librarian, I figured out the country code and began furiously dialing random numbers. Eventually I got someone. I was disappointed when the voice responded, "Hello."

In college, I went through a phase of calling my parents at odd hours and saying I was with the IRS or the FBI or the CIA or the local police, whatever could get struggling immigrants on political asylum really going. The time difference was fascinating to me—for once I could beat them to the day. I was good at doing voices and they weren't used to hearing mine from far away, so it went quite well. When their troubles and mine both grew and there was no space for fake emergencies, I stopped.

While waiting for the *New York Times* review, I began crank-calling my friends with the assistance of my boyfriend. We had characters. We called famous people, professional contacts. Some never found out who it was. One friend went so far as to pay for tracking the number. He was, to put it mildly, pissed. When my best friend heard from him, she was pissed. They both left messages that eerily employed the same sentence: "We're fucking thirty."

To this day, I have not patched up things with about half a dozen victims of the Great *New York Times Book Review* Waiting Period. The review was good in the end, but I lost friends I'd had for more than twenty years. What do you say? How do you explain it?

7. Portrait of the Starving Artist

October 2007: It is a fact that even a *NYTBR*-approved novelist can still find herself in highly undignified positions at certain times. Two months later, I am sitting Indian-style on the dirty linoleum floor at the JFK Delta baggage claim, hugging my carry-on bag like it's a pillow and trying to sob subtly into my cell phone.

I'm crying about money, something I have a negative amount of, according to a robot at my bank. I have some change in my jacket, but it is not even enough for a cookie from the concession stand in front of me, and I am starving.

I haven't had money for weeks. My paperwork for my new job at the university has not gone through. My publisher has paid for some plane flights and hotels, but I have not had more than what a struggling boyfriend could spare. I have a million fancy dresses to wear and a lot of good face to put on, but all I've been doing is eyeing the prices on every menu and pretending cookies and chips are my foods of choice, that Subway is my adorably ironic passion, that the McDonald's breakfast menu is my kitschy little crush.

But the most disturbing part of my overdrafting then is that it largely resulted from a certain check, made out in the summer, that I have no memory of. It is a three-figure check, written out to . . . *my psychic.*

I call people, but I don't want to ask for help. I want them to think of it as a humorous anecdote, but not that it's real, that my life is that difficult. After all, certain friends who are not involved in publishing think I am rich and famous. Why burst that bubble?

I do end up borrowing money from a friend of my boy-friend's and take a walk of shame to a yellow cab, when I know there are buses and shuttles and subways and all sorts of ways to get back to Brooklyn.

Later, when my publicist finds out, she is shocked. "Why didn't you call us?!"

I give her some gloss-over answer, but I want to say, *I don't know who to call, when to call, why to call.* I am learning everything over again. I have become what the publishing world and media suspect of a debut novelist—suddenly I am new to the universe, not just to being a novelist. I don't know what the hell I'm doing.

Weeks later, I discover during another bad moment—as the value of the dollar plummets and oil is sky-high—that gold is at its peak value. I sell what is left of the family heir-looms in my care to an old Iranian man in the Diamond District, who listens to a fraction of my story, gives me a decent deal, and tells me, "My boy in medical university; my girl, married and with baby. Your fault for being a starver of an artist, daughter."

8. Portrait of an Artist with a Crazy Name, and Also Crazy Hair

There is the issue of my name, of course. To everyone who is not Dr. or Mrs. Khakpour, it is insurmountable—the ulti-mate hyperethnic polysyllabic foreign name, even foreign to "my people," who rarely recognize its Zoroastrian origin, the name of Zarathushtra's daughter: Pourucista. My last name is the same as a famous Iranian soccer player—Mohammad, no relation—so people can handle it. It means *of the earth*, literally *dirt-full*.

No one can say it, and I even say it differently, depending on the person. In Farsi, it is best uttered in a low purr: *Poe-roh-chis-TAWH KHAK-pur*. Americans—unless they speak Hebrew—are often disappointed to find out this is indeed the guttural *kh*, requiring more gut than a German *ich*.

My name is a mess of issues that I have swept under the Iranian-American carpet, over and over and over, until I have forgotten it's there.

Until publication season, that is. Then I start really hearing and seeing my own name again. It bends into its old bizarre forms: *Porchista, Prochista, Parochista, Kahkpour, Kkakpour, Khapour*, plus some I have never heard. People make fun of it like they did in elementary school; my book party gets linked on Gawker, and one of the first comments is the easiest: "Khakpour. I made that sound this morning before my first cigarette and coughed up last night's tequila binge."

Two months later, I go to a literary party in New York, and Gawker takes a shot of me drunkenly smiling. A commentator refers to me as "that Barista Kockpour." Nancy's Baby Names, a website created by a Harvard grad "to provide helpful, entertaining information to expectant parents," includes me in her list of "some unusual real names for the weekend." I appear alongside literary critic Cleanth Brooks, British archaeologist Jacquetta Hawkes, diplomat Spruille Braden, and sixteenth-century Dutch Haarlem governor Wigbolt Ripperda, as "Porochista Khakpour, Iranian-American writer."

Before an interview at NPR, Kurt Andersen asks me how

to pronounce my name, and I tell him. When we're on the air, he does the opposite of those who fumble it, who say it quietly and quickly, almost under their breath, like a bad thought they want to go away soon. He belts it! My first name is on target—go, Kurt, go!—but my last name is *KHHHHAWK-por*, which exactly rhymes with, say, "rock whore." Katherine Lanpher, the fill-in host of *The Leonard Lopate Show*, turns it into the Mexi-Minneapolitan *"Poew-rrrow-chista Khakpowr."* An Iranian Voice of America anchor, meanwhile, nails the last name but turns the first into *Prochesta*, a pronunciation that Iranians sadly seem to favor. Reading series hosts all fumble, and one even christens me *Chalkpore*. And of course many opt for what is still the general consensus among my closest hometown friends: *Hawkpurr*.

When people to whom I have to be nice fudge the damn thing, I smile, laugh, nod to make them feel comfortable, shake my head, roll my eyes jokingly, add a smile, and with a wave of my hand, give them the magic panacea: "Call me whatever you want, I've heard it all."

They feel better.

I didn't change my name and never will. But one way I have battled the drama of a difficult name is with other distractions. I've had piercings, tattoos, hair of every shade, cuts from nearly shaved to ass-length braided extensions. Just before my literary shit hits the fan, I ask my hairdresser to Cruella de Vil my hair, to "ugly me up."

"Tough," he responds, racing both tattooed hands through my thick, black, disgustingly pretty hair.

"Totally fucked up," I elaborate. "A little badass, kinda burly. Y'know?"

People notice. Style.com applauds my "skunk-style high-lights" and my "deliberately down-market look." A writer for ParsArts, a young Iranian arts site, declares "my fascination with her as an author is slowly being overcome by a fascination with her hair." The name disappears a bit.

9. Superpowers

After my readings, I generally get some people who just want to talk. This is fine with me. I like comp lit students, and I can stomach the occasional housewife who wonders if I've ever read a book called *The Kite Runner*, by a guy whose name she "forgets" (i.e., can't say), which she read to know more about "us."

The other group is not as easy—they appear to be average middle-aged white males, but that's just a Clark Kent cover. They are really conspiracy-theory superheroes! They have seen the shadow of the World Trade Center in front of my novel and know I am Middle Eastern, and they have their own ideas about my religion, and so they want to share with me "the truth about 9/11." I politely decline going down that road every time, and still they carry on. Eventually I excuse myself to visit the bathroom and put on my own super-hero getup, my Invisible Snakegirl tube suit, which allows me to slither away undetected from even the most tenacious leeches.

But sometimes it doesn't work out. At one of the final readings on my tour, an older man maybe senses my impatience and murmurs, "Anyway, in a coupla months it's suicide for me."

10. For a Limited Time Only: Mahmoud Ahmadinejad Included in the Portrait

On the afternoon of September 24, 2007, Iranian president Mahmoud Ahmadinejad, en route to addressing the United Nations General Assembly, gave a speech at Columbia University. It was a big deal.

Less of a big deal to the world, but a big deal to me, was the next day: my technical publication date. One day after that, my first book club appearance; three days later, the first day of my book tour. In all my interactions, the theme was Ahmadinejad.

One woman at a reading whispered in my ear, "Iran is hot—lucky you!"

I fake-laughed. What a gas. The Senate passed a resolution designating a whole branch of the Iranian military a terrorist organization, giving our American president the authority to let games begin with Iran, and I am *lucky*?

At almost every reading, someone inevitably raises her hand and utters, "So, Ahmadinejad . . . ?"

For a few weeks, I smile and nod. "Yes, *Mah-moooood Ahmadeeeee-nezhaad*"—deep Farsi phonetics—"my homeland's president. Well . . ." Every reading provides a challenge to say something comforting yet not bland, aware yet not activist, polished but not sharp. It gets old quick. I start wanting to ask people, *Can't we talk about anything else? 9/11, anyone?!* It's a bad sign when you have to wish for 9/11 as an icebreaker.

At readings later that autumn, I become what Iranians call a *bacheyeh powrooh,* which translates as "kid full of spirit," or a rather rude child. So I quip in response, "What about him?"

"Well," says the nervously smiling American, looking down at her sneakers, "what do you think of all this?"

In my imagination, I am Picasso declaring, "I don't," when asked what he thought of the man on the moon. But in real life, humor—with a flushed face—is the only route I can take.

"I never dated Mahmoud Ahmadinejad and therefore have no insight into what he's like, what he's thinking."

But this American does not like that answer. "But certainly . . . ?"

I smile, not unlike Ahmadinejad himself, and say, "Imagine I see what you see."

The American smiles back and sits down, done.

11. Portrait Now

After everything, I give up and dye my hair black, my natural color.

After a few months of this old black, as fake now as it was real then, they come in bunches not unlike streaks. Not one, not two, but many and counting, early and yet expected, perfectly white hairs.

Part Two

*

Thirteen Ways
of Being an Immigrant

1

The year is 1983 and Cabbage Patch Kids are at the height
of their popularity. You want one but you know your parents
can't afford it. A couple of years into living in this country and
they keep telling you they will go back to Iran soon—that the
war will be over, that the revolution will be done, that you
will be a refugee and alien no more. But for now, there is little
money. At school, you know you are one of the few kids with
less access to things and you know the others are not from
here, either. You work with them to get out of ESL and you
try to act like kids who belong here, who have money. One
way to do this is to have a Cabbage Patch Kid doll, but this
seems impossible. Still, your mother takes you to Toys"R"Us,

which seems like the greatest place on earth, second only to Disneyland, which you've only heard about, since it also costs too much to go. At Toys"R"Us, several aisles are devoted to the Cabbage Patch dolls—if it were a farm, this area would be the Cabbage Patch. Their chubby faces peer at you from behind the plastic of their boxes. You have not considered which one you want because you don't think you will ever get one. Maybe an imitation at some point, one without a signature on the butt, which is how you've heard you know they are real; true Cabbage Patch Kids, the real ones, come with butt tattoos. You are looking at them longingly, when your mother points to a section down the aisle. There is a big sign: SALE. There is a whole section of Cabbage Patch Kids on sale, it turns out, and your mother is telling you they are in her budget, but she doesn't think they are the right ones for you. You are elated, then confused—why would she think that? And then you look at them, one by one, row after row. What do they have in common? They are black, all of them, the ones on sale. You think about it. They could be your adopted child, why not? You are still too young to know how babies are made, so you don't think much deeper. You reach out to a pig-tailed black one in a yellow tracksuit and you tell your mother that this is your daughter. Her name turns out to be Clover Stephanie, and you still have her somewhere in storage. Her cheek is a bit scraped and it looks white underneath. It bothers you, that fact. It bothers you also that you have Clover only because she was on sale, because she was black, but that was an important first lesson about America, so maybe it was worth it.

2

You want to be a good student, the best in fact. One way to do this is to follow directions. In kindergarten, this is a big goal of yours, since English is still new to you. One rule is that, at lunchtime, you must eat your dessert last. Dessert is usually a piece of fruit, but apparently it is hard for the kids to obey this rule. Not you. You always get it right. Your best friend is a blond girl named Angela, whom all the teachers love. She doesn't always play by the rules, but she always gets away with it. One day she eats her cantaloupe before her spaghetti. This shocks you. You try to tell her to stop it, that she can't do this, but she does it. Without any fear, a smile even. You tell her to stop or you will have to tell on her. She smiles with a mouth full of cantaloupe. She is fearless. You tell her to stop right now, because you are truly about to tell. She laughs, more cantaloupe on her tongue. You can't take it anymore. You tell on her. The teaching assistant is a big man named Mr. Mondo and he is tough on the rules. He will take care of this. You walk right up to him and as much as it pains you, you point right at her. "Angela is eating her dessert first, Mr. Mondo." At this point, Angela is still, a look of fright on her face. She is not taunting you anymore. *Good*, you think, *this might teach her*. Mr. Mondo walks with you to her. He asks her if she did it. She nods sadly. "Sorry," she says. He says nothing and pauses. Then he turns to you and he looks angry. He says one word: "snitcher." He walks away and Angela smiles and you begin to cry and—after you learn what that word means, though from the start you know it's bad—once again you learn a lesson about America.

3

Your best friend in second grade lives in the good part of town. So does almost everyone at your elementary school. You live in the bad part of town. No one you know lives there. Your dad drives a Pinto while your best friend's dad drives a Rolls-Royce. She hates it. You go to her house. It is a mansion in the hills. She has so many expensive toys— numerous Cabbage Patch dolls, all white, even though she is Vietnamese. She was born in America, unlike you. Her dad drives a truck for a living while yours is a professor. Another lesson, you one day realize.

4

The usual substitute teacher, the one everyone in your grade sees most often, makes funny jokes, and one is that he calls you "my Iranian sweetheart." You hate this, because you know Americans don't like Iran and you don't want to be singled out and teased—especially not because of being Iranian. But he always does this. Another teacher sticks his thumb in your mouth when he spots you sticking your tongue out at a friend. You don't know what it means, but it feels wrong. Years later, a science teacher offers you massages after class. You decline. A few grades down, a German teacher tells you you are so beautiful—he whispers it to you and you never come near him again. That same year a librarian tells you about male and female plugs too eagerly, demonstrating over and over. Another teacher laughs when students say you look like Anne Frank and makes a joke about him looking like a German soldier. You remember his bad breath on your face as he laughs at you, all over you. "Are there Jews still in Iran?" he asks you, but you don't answer. In America, adults are inappropriate, you realize—maybe a lesson about this place, but maybe not.

5

You became editor in chief of your high school paper, your one and only dream in life as you so far know it. For two years, you have this post. You love nothing more. When your adviser is fired—a gay man—you are incensed and you walk out and your staff follows. You are now seen as a rebel. This somehow seems very American. Your fearlessness also seems very American. You are blond Angela with the cantaloupe. You must belong here if you think you can afford to leave.

6

You go to college in New York—your dream—and you get your first internship at *The Village Voice*. You are a teenager and a scholarship kid and you have no money, and it does not occur to you that students ask their parents for money. You are left wondering how you can make this work, so you learn to jump trains. Another scholarship kid teaches you. You get good at this—you go to your internship three times a week and use some change for dinner: Pop-Tarts from the vending machine. And then you jump the train back. Part of it is you must look well-dressed to do this. You pretend you are dressing up for your internship. But you are doing it because they suspect you less if you look fancy. One time you get caught. A female conductor. She tells you she's been watching you for months. You have no money to give her, so she tells you your luck is up and she's kicking you off. It's midnight and the stop is Mount Vernon, a bad neighborhood. You are let out there and an old man offers you a drive home. You have no other choice. You stop jumping trains.

7

Sometimes you stay out all night. You miss the last train back to college upstate on purpose, knowing the next one is at six a.m. No worries. The clubs are open all night. You go to them and lose yourself in them. In America, you fit in at clubs more than anywhere else. They are for you. It's there that people accept you the most. Very little matters in the forever night of a club, and you learn then to trust darkness more than light.

8

You go on your year abroad to Oxford. You joke that you are doing it to dry out from drugs and drinking, but this is somewhat true. But there you find more clubs and more drugs and drinking. They call you American Express, that group of boys you sleep with. You're amazed they call you American.

9

At age nineteen, you are raped. At age twenty, you are raped again. This strikes you as something that happens to American girls, a rite of passage. You tell no one, which American girls seem to do, too, or not do.

10

You see 9/11 outside your East Village window, and you remember your first nightmares as a recent immigrant in the eighties. Men in dark clothing with machine guns and machetes loose on your city streets. They were terrorists and you were the hostages. In your dream, it's always in Iran. In your dream, you are safe in America. But not in reality, you realize. Your old world has come for you. *This is what being an American looks like now*, you think as you take your shoes off in an airport security line for the first time.

11

You become a published author. An American author. No, an Iranian-American author. Never does the hyphen matter more than when you are an author, it seems.

12

In your teens, you contemplate suicide. In your twenties, you contemplate suicide. In your thirties, you contemplate suicide. Before turning forty, you wonder how many more times you will contemplate suicide. You wonder if you'd have been happier in that other life you were meant to live: the one where you stayed in Iran and maybe got married and had kids and maybe never became a writer. Maybe you would already have died of suicide.

13

You are nineteen years an American—you became an American in November 2001—and you realize you could have had a child in that time. You have no kids, no husband, no home you own, no roots. No real reason to be here. Trump becomes president and your old country is on the list of one of the six countries of the "Muslim ban." You are suddenly a Muslim. No one doubts your brownness anymore. You realize that every day is a lesson in America, the real America, the violent one. You remember blond Angela with the cantaloupe glistening in her laughing mouth and you think, for the first time, she was maybe laughing at you. Why would you think you'd get anywhere? On Facebook, you beg your white friends to do better, you ask them for ideas on where to live, you try to imagine another future they have. You wonder if your Americanness is forever and if you will die an American. You realize it might be just as hard to shake being an American as it was to become one in the first place. You realize with joy that you will die an American; you realize with agony you will die an American; you realize with horror and confusion and fear and disbelief that you will die an American. Somehow it is harder to imagine than dying.

Secret Muslims
in the New Year

March 2017 is the first March of my life that I've had to be reminded of Persian New Year.

At my local dog park in Harlem, on an unseasonably hot day, as my standard poodle buddied up to an old Siberian husky, the white owner and I broke into the usual dog talk. Dog names first, then ours. I said my name slowly, though it came out softer than I'd hoped, and I searched the woman's eyes.

She said, *Beautiful name, what is it?* I'd heard that sentence my whole life, so I blurted it out with rehearsed confidence: *Iranian.*

Between us, a mess of ellipses, the sound of basketballs on courts, a distant siren, a tangle of dog barks. *What does it mean?* And my usual: *It's an ancient Zoroastrian name, an unusual one for Iranians.*

I thought to explain to her that I'm of Muslim background, but instead I just hoped for the awkward parting of people whose only connection is canines. She looked deep in thought and I thought maybe she felt sorry for me—Iranian in a time of Trump's Muslim ban, after all—but maybe she felt her own discomfort.

She cut into my ruminations with a question I didn't expect: *Isn't your New Year coming soon?*

I was astounded more than anything by the realization that I'd forgotten this holiday of holidays. I gave the stranger a flustered thank-you.

How did she know that? What did that stranger really think? A pause. *What exactly am I afraid of?*

❋

Persian New Year, or Nowruz, is a celebration of spring. It falls at the exact time of the vernal equinox, which shifts in accordance with axial precession. Weeks before it happens, every Iranian I know excitedly looks up the time online and plans a day around it. This is not a holiday we take lightly.

The celebration is thousands of years old, with roots in ancient Indo-Persian culture, in a religion some say the prophet Zoroaster created. Nowruz means "new day," its spiritual origin extended to secular appreciation by all sorts of people who can claim some ancient Persian origin, including, of course, modern-day Iranians.

These days, many Instagram accounts all over the world have turned Nowruz traditions into cult obsessions. Nothing gives good photo like the table-setting haftsin, an arrangement of seven foods beginning with *s*: sprouts (sabzeh), wheat pudding (samanu), dried oleaster (senjed), garlic (sir), apples (seeb), vinegar (serkeh), and sumac fruit (somāq). All this is skirted with springlike paraphernalia such as candies, eggs, mirrors, flowers, and even goldfish. One could argue Iranians worship beauty, and it's never more apparent than in Nowruz aesthetics.

My favorite memories of Nowruz involve my trying to derail my mother's efforts in beautifying our Nowruz. The profound mischief of altering the haftsin without my parents noticing was a great goal of mine—one time, at age six or seven, I tried to drown a hairless Barbie in the goldfish bowl. Often I'd try to pollute the immaculate individual haftsin bowls with Cheerios and M&M's, anything obviously American. But I also relished the cultural "abnormalities" that could feel like American transgressions—for instance, my parents waking us up in the middle of the night on a school night to celebrate tahvil sal, the exact moment of equinox, a given no matter what horrible hour it came.

We grew up with few luxuries, so I was excited for the treats we received at Nowruz. We were to wear new clothes that day, and that meant we would visit the mall, where I could make a case for some impractical Contempo Casuals creation. *We have to do it for Persia!* I'd cry, waving some lacy tube top on sale. All sorts of luxurious-seeming foods appeared at our table. Persian cookies—walnut, almond, rice, raisin—from the grocery stores in L.A.'s "Little Persia" were my favorite. Later, in college, my parents sent care packages full of them, and I boasted to friends that these were Persian comfort foods. Everything smelled of rosewater, cardamom, pistachio, and saffron—and even I could not resist Nowruz's embarrassment of glamour.

Most of all, in my youth I believed Nowruz might have the power to eclipse the kinds of things that were said about my homeland on television and in the news. I hoped the imagery of beauty and hope and optimism could eclipse it.

❊

In 2017, Nowruz fell at half past six in the morning for me. I've never been the best early riser, but I know the hour well these days; since the 2016 election, my nights were a mess of anxiety-induced insomnia keeping me up close to dawn. Early in the morning, my dog took to waking me up with a sermon of barks—a new habit.

I realized my 110-unit turn-of-the-century Harlem building had its share of early morning visitors. Nine deportations, a neighbor reports to me, while another says less and another many more, while another tells me not to talk about this. My building happens to be mostly Muslim—brown, black, and white Muslim—and is located close to several prominent mosques, one of the reasons I've loved living here. But in the hallway, my neighbors and I wonder what others are saying. In hushed tones, we curse the casual and constant bigotry of this administration, just as we beg one another to take good care.

We residents have become closer since the 2015 Paris

terror attacks, when police presence in this neighborhood ramped up noticeably. Before that, many of us didn't know where we stood, who we were—you can't always tell who is Muslim, after all. None of our names sounded like the stereotypes, none of us fit a profile made by Islamophobes. There was the maintenance guy from Montenegro, the waitress of Lebanese origin, the Turkish couple, the Egyptian siblings, the old black Muslim families who've been in Harlem for decades, the other Iranian woman, a student, and, of course, me.

For the last few years, I've been joking I'm a Secret Muslim. Iranian nationalism and exceptionalism always steered my father far away from discussions of Islam. Nowruz was a time for him to wave his old Iranian flag (the one with the lion and sword, not the one of the Islamic Republic), to color-copy and frame Persepolis photos from library books, to present me and my brother with the fake gold Zoroastrian-iconographic pins. *The great Persian empire!* he'd cry in his little moldy apartment with the decaying carpet, surrounded by sometimes-hostile neighbors.

That same father took us to Zoroastrian temples in Orange County. I never understood why we got such dirty looks until I was past my teens and realized we'd only been religious tourists at their temples. We were never Zoroastrian, and we couldn't be. The religion was dying—some say less than 150,000 remain—because you have to be born into it. But its old traditions, like Nowruz, have retained their influence in cultures of the region. Muslim Iranians tend to look to Zoroastrianism with pride.

But when my father sought to gild my identity with a Zoroastrian name, it wasn't because of cultural pride; it took me years to realize maybe he thought it was a form of protection. When he'd stop my late grandmother from reciting verses from the Koran in public, maybe it wasn't shame for his cultural origins—maybe he just didn't trust Americans to hear it.

❋

In 2017, I wanted to forget Nowruz. Even in my circle of Iranian friends in New York, I heard us beginning to plan but thinking twice in a way we never had before. *Not in the mood*, one friend told me. *Not in the mood*, I told another friend. And I thought about how my parents and I were barely in contact then—all of us were locked in our own suffering.

Naturalized at twenty-three, I thought about how my birthplace is still on my passport, in bold letters: *Iran*. I thought about my father back home in L.A. with only a green card. I thought about the old traumas and the usual traumas, all the times I've been pulled aside at airports way before this era of the Muslim ban, and the newer traumas, daily online harassment such as: "go back to whatever Third World shithole you come from."

I remembered the Nowruzes I celebrated with my family when I was young.

For me, no matter where I was or when it was, there was spring, and there was Nowruz. Even as my family changed, Nowruz anchored us to the old within the new.

It was not an easy holiday, though.

Nowruz 1363 (1984). The tahvil sal—the vernal equinox—fell around three a.m. We had moved to South

Pasadena. My mother frantically stripped my brother and me of our pajamas and put on newly purchased T-shirts, as part of Nowruz tradition is to wear something new at the exact hour of its commencement. I was crazy-eyed and delirious and grumpy. Why couldn't we celebrate a holiday like normal Americans, at the same time each year, at a good honest midnight? On the TV, the music (too heart-wrenching and drummy and hard to ignore) and the dancing (too sexy and fancy and hard to ignore) seemed both foreign and familiar, a startling combination.

Nowruz 1369 (1990). We were on a Sequoia National Park road trip, in my father's non-air-conditioned and radio-free hatchback, and stopped for a late lunch at a Marie Callender's in Bakersfield, California. There we had tahvil sal among ham stacks, country-fried steak, and razzleberry pie. This was how I imagined Dorothy's Kansas family ate.

My mother and my father tried to enlist us in a silly song about the new year and my brother complained that he was carsick even though he wasn't in the car—all in loud Persian. I realized the dining room, everyone pink-faced except us, had gone silent, looking our way. I, the self-conscious pre-teen, shushed my family. Perhaps Nowruz should be kept in the house.

Norwuz 1373, my first sizdah bedar, the celebration marking the thirteenth day of the new year, was to be spent outside, preferably in nature, a requirement anathema to the depressive, indoorsy geek I had grown into. Huge flocks of Iranians gathered at parks and picnicked to ward off unlucky thirteen. Young women tied knots in blades of grass, a gesture of making a wish for a husband. Relatives made elaborate jokes of nudging grass at me, a premature spinster at a salty sixteen, my mustache and hairy legs fluorescent emblems of forever virginhood.

✳

I tried to imagine skipping Nowruz altogether; I tried to imagine giving in to grief as an opportunity to meditate on the horrors of this era.

And as I tried to let go of Nowruz, it came for me. A neighbor's card appeared at my door: *Happy 1396, we are with you*, reads the cursive. Later I found myself scrolling through the Instagram accounts of families in Tehran and I marveled at their haftsin skills. I caught myself dreaming of a last-minute gathering.

At the dog park, the stranger with the Siberian husky appears again, and we chat about the promise of new blooms, our worries of climate change, the complications that separate and connect us. *Happy New Year*, we say to each other, *Nowruz Mobarak*. She reveals to me that she taught in Iran long ago, and I realize she knows the hospital where I was born and has been to my mother's hometown, that she remembers skiing on a day like this in the mountains there.

We walk together and laugh at how our dogs can't stop licking the mounds of gray city ice.

Born-Again Carnivorism

1987, Pasadena, California

Five years into living in the United States, my family cel-
ebrates our first Thanksgiving. I can see my mother tack-
ling her first turkey in the kitchen when I, nine years old,
walk in—a moment not unlike when a child walks in on
her parents having sex. *We are* eating *that?* I ask, pointing
to the white goose-pimpled thing, nothing like what I saw
in commercials, which featured tan, glazed, muscular entrees
like diet program *After* photos. Later that evening we gather
around it, laid out on a red plaid tablecloth, with paper cups
full of Ocean Spray cranberry juice cocktail, while my father
takes pictures, the first of many photos we have from family

Thanksgivings where I look like an adolescent clinical depression poster girl.

At a defiant fifteen, I've had it. The first milestone of my teen years is River Phoenix's death, and when the news emphasizes his vegetarianism, I have that aha moment. Could it be that my problem is the food of the man? MEAT?!

The dinner table is the perfect setting for my first move of adult independence: *I am now a vegetarian, parents.*

My horrified mother bombards me with a jumble of facts and fictions: *meat makes you tall and strong; meat makes you live longer; meat makes you beautiful* (her most potent weapon). She is panicked as the cook of the house, since Iranian cuisine is an unabashedly carnivorous one. There are vegetables, but they come mostly in the form of herbs—they are garnish, adornment, afterthought. My mother's usual weekly menu is a steady rotation of koofteh (Persian meatballs, basically), beef kebab, and various meat stews. Therefore my vegetarianism is certainly destined to be a fissure in a fraught mother-daughter relationship. Meanwhile, my father, less worried, coolly mumbles that he was a vegetarian once, but it was *a phase.*

My herbivore love affair was lusty. A first-grade questionnaire reveals that my "favorite food" was "*SALLAD.*" To this day I can't imagine starting the day without a variety of green leafy things in the blender: my beloved green juices. *Hay and cud,* my mother always grumbled, seeing it as a teenage rebellion I wouldn't outgrow. *Don't come running to me when being a cow kills you.*

2010, Santa Fe, New Mexico

And then it does: I seem healthy for most of my life until 2010. I move to Santa Fe in late summer and notice prolonged high-altitude discomfort. A visit to the doctor's office reveals that I am not just anemic, as I had suspected, but have the lowest blood sugar my doctor has ever seen and very low insulin. Adrenal and pancreatic tumors, diabetes type 2 and then diabetes type 1, polycystic ovary syndrome, and celiac disease are all possibilities. My diet is probed, and while I go on about my green juices, some other details are revealed: entire weeks of potato salad lunches, whole boxes of pasta as dinner-for-one servings, a daily allegiance to beers of the stout and porter variety. She denounces me as a carb and sugar addict, demands an urgent end to all of it, and finally utters one word that is to become my fate: *paleo*. The trendy caveman diet of animal protein, fat, and veggies is to be my new gastro-religion. For minutes, we argue—from ethics (*I rescue dogs!*) to romantics (*my new fiancé is vegan!*)—but she tells me my life depends on it, so that's the end of that.

Overnight, I am reborn as a carnivore. There I am at the grocery store choosing cuts of meat with the awkwardness of a man selecting panty hose for his wife. At restaurants, I feel mistaken for an Atkins-crazed trophy wife, ordering bunless this and riceless that, and I crumble under overly empathetic looks from other women as I pass on dessert. Plus, I have to endure watching my fiancé enjoy all the heartbeat-less eats we once shared. *It seems all we have in common now are some vegetables*, I glumly tell my parents over the phone.

Meat makes you beautiful, my mother repeats, as if I'm fifteen again.

2011, Los Angeles, California

There is meat and then there is *meat.* Of the latter variety, kaleh pacheh is king. It's what renowned Persian chef Najmieh Batmanglij translates to lamb's head and feet stew—just what it sounds like: a whole sheep head with eyeballs, tongue, and brains, as well as hooves, all stewed for hours in water, onions, and garlic. This is a breakfast meal Iranians often eat before dawn. Anecdotal lore indicates that grandmothers and aunts generally tackle this for the sake of their men, who, my father hypothesizes, bond over it as a "macho thing." My mother has always boasted a love of it; I have feared it my entire life.

When I return home for the first time in years, more extreme forms of meat-eating jokingly surface among the family, and then so does the ultimate bogeyman: kaleh pacheh.

My father is the first to voice dread. Apparently, his older sister had almost run away from home when their mother tried to make it. *If you try it, I don't want to know,* he insists.

But I argue that it's hypocritical of us to be digging into a drumstick and then drawing the line at a head or a hoof. I mean, what animal parts do hot dogs come from? If I am going meatward, I might as well look my meat in the eye: *literally.*

My mother is an easy in. After flirting with the idea of

making it (*I will move out*, my father threatens), she suggests a few cafés that offer servings, most famously Westwood's Canary Restaurant, and so we head over for a late breakfast.

The Specials section of Canary's menu is an extravagant resting place of Iranian extreme cuisine: heart, kidney, liver, halem (*imagine if oatmeal included ground turkey*, my mother explains), donbalan (lamb testicles, politely left description-less on the menu), sirabee (lamb stomach lining soup), and, of course, kaleh pacheh. Our waitress—a young, wisecracking Tehrangelina—winces when she sees us two ladies—my mother in a cardigan and pearls, me in a dress and heels—order stomach soup, testicle apps, and head and hoof stew.

We begin with the plate of small pinkish balls, unmistakable in their plain-as-naked-day visuals. My mother polishes off two with enviable ease; I manage a shaky forkful of a half, and fortunately it's sausage-like enough to remind you of, well, sausage.

Silence, sighs. My mother smiles sweetly, I smile sweetly back, but behind the smiles, we are cowboys at a showdown. Who will put their utensils down first?

We got to do the kaleh pacheh fast, while it lasts, my mother finally breaks the silence. *It goes to . . . jelly.*

Congeals?

My mother nods bleakly; I nod at the face in my bowl.

As we poke around with our spoons, the waitress pops up, reading the thing like a map—*that's eyeball, that's tongue, that's definitely brains.* For a while I just take spoonfuls of the broth—mildly creamy with a surprising tanginess. I refuse to think too hard about the source of the tang. Eventually, after witnessing my mother relish her brains, I slice into some tongue. Its texture: traumatizingly tonguey. Its taste: generically meaty. My feeling: badass.

Sirabee is last, but not least. It's a greenish soup of thick yellow ribbons that could have been tagliatelle if you are as invested in denial as I am. The smell, something else. When I finally go for it, it is just a weird, bitter, rubbery soup. My mother's first misstep, a near gag, gives me the advantage—finally a dish I have her beat on.

Still, I have to tip my hat to her for putting down the bulk of the meal, this woman whose whole life has been nonfat fad diets. And I imagine her hat-tip to me for going where no vegetarian has gone: offal.

On the drive home, we sit full and exhausted in a heavy silence, like homebound soldiers. We have eaten something with a face—we have eaten its face actually. We are black-belt meateaters. For a second I have an out-of-body feeling. How did I become this person? How did some hiccups with my health turn into a life of animal sacrifices? I coat all the queasy in my stomach and heart with the resignation of a war general—this is my new path and I have to take it. And yet, bizarrely enough, later that night, it's my mother who says, *How about vegetarian for dinner?* At Green Earth Vegan in Pasadena, where my mother wolfs down her "soy chick'un salad" and I my stew of pumpkin, eggplant, and tofu, we give silent thanks at the altar of the herbivorism, where nothing congeals and haunts, where the only hearts and guts to conquer are inside us.

On Becoming a
Middle Eastern–American

In the late nineties and early aughts, I used to frequent a boutique in the East Village called Michael and Hushi. Hushi Mortezaie, an impish club kid born in Iran and raised in the Bay Area, made outlandish, psychedelic, robot-chic clothing and was getting the coolest of the East Village cool kids to wear his strategically slashed and torn Farsi-graffitied shirts, though few of them had any idea that in some cases they were sporting post–Iranian Revolution political slogans.

I used to go to downtown parties in a skimpy halter top that featured newsprint-emblazoned mujahideen women brandishing machine guns, their bullets bedazzled in gold next to the words "Long Live Iran." I loved the feeling of being able to be Iranian and play on it at the same time.

In one of the last days of August 2001, I remember visiting the boutique again. Hushi was giddy preparing for Fashion Week. His store windows were freshly adorned with his "Persian collection," a new line of hijab-and-harem-pant Iranophilia. "Girl, get ready!" he said. "Iran is going to be the new black."

Days later, there we were, two Middle Eastern twenty-somethings who now had some explaining to do. Friends started speaking in roundabout inquiries: What exactly *was* the status of my green card? How *were* my father and brother faring? Were they Muslim, by the way?

Hushi's stylists, meanwhile, were calling him to ask how he was—and when he was going to be getting rid of that window display. But somehow we were fine enough, even under the heavy air of everyone's condescending concern.

Almost a full decade after 9/11, more anti-Muslim xenophobia emerged, fully formed and fever-pitched, ostensibly over plans to build an interfaith cultural center near Ground Zero. Even in New York, stronghold of progressive ethics and cultural diversity, my longtime home.

In addition to the issue surrounding the mosque, a Florida pastor wanted to burn Korans on the September 11 anniversary, and who has yes-no-maybe-so reconsidered, after a hearty load of negative press and a dab of headshaking. Then a drunk white college student, who had actually been to Afghanistan, stabbed a Bangladeshi Muslim in a cab.

For the record: back then, I did not identify as Muslim. My immediate family raised my brother and me as agnostic as possible. My mother prayed to a guardian angel and my dad "studied" Zoroastrianism. But most of the extended Khakpours are Muslim, and culturally, it's always been a part of me.

I am also a New Yorker. When 9/11 happened, I had just moved into a studio twenty-five floors up, with a nearly all-glass wall that framed a perfect view of the World Trade Center.

Now, when I look back on ages twenty-three to thirty-two, every aspect of my life is shadowed by what I saw through the glass that Tuesday morning: two towers, each gashed and hazed in the glitter of exploding windows, falling, one after the other. But what was once simple apprehension and mortification and trepidation became increasingly entangled with feelings of exhaustion and marginalization and indignation.

✳

Just six days after 9/11, at the Islamic Center of Washington, President Bush said: "Those who feel like they can intimidate our fellow citizens to take out their anger don't represent the best of America, they represent the worst of humankind." He added: "The face of terror is not the true faith of Islam. That's not what Islam is all about. Islam is peace." Did that assurance mean more to white Americans having come from someone who looked like them?

Xenophobia and racism abounded. For conservatives, people of color, along with all our white liberal friends, were lumped together in one misery-loves-company fringe. In the Obama years, conservatives positioned themselves as aggrieved victims. I recall the advice of an older female relative: *Always let men you're in relationships with have all the power; it's when they lose power and get insecure that your problems start.*

Indeed, during Obama's administration, 9/11 payback

resurfaced precisely because we elected an African-American president whose middle name—the name of cousins of mine—was turned into an H-word slur. A Fort Hood gunman, a would-be Times Square bomber, and the controversy over the "Ground Zero mosque" made for a boiling hot summer of anti-Islamic assault. Anyone with skin as dark as President Obama's could be a "secret Muslim," and any Muslim must surely be a not-so-secret terrorist.

The world Hushi and I were in, before 9/11 and just after, was not a picnic for brown people. None of us breathed easy. It's just that we expected to breathe easier as time went on.

❋

My brother, who used to live in Brooklyn, discovered that many of his Muslim friends in New York felt that the construction of an Islamic cultural center by Ground Zero was a bad idea to begin with, for this sole reason: it was going to put them in danger. He and his friends were afraid.

During our late-night calls, my brother and I talked about nothing but what was on the news, and we laughed a lot, but we laughed nervously. My sense of humor, honed in my immigrant childhood, was my disarming mechanism, a handy way to infuse the blues with some off color.

My humor curdled at the moment I was feeling the most euphoric: during Obama's bid for the presidency. I started murdering whole days in the dirty basement of the Internet, the comments sections of blogs. There an angry tribe of fake names spoke in misspelled obscenities and declaimed the true evil nature of Middle Easterners and their intentions in this country. This is silly, I'd tell myself, these trolls aren't representative of my neighbors or of Americans.

Then I'd go on Facebook and engage in more online warfare with friends of friends, real flesh-and-blood people with real-life names, who a bit more politely and grammatically stated the same. And there was me—a non-Muslim, who has publicly criticized certain Islamic practices—flaccidly battling for Muslims worldwide. It got to the point that I was telling people I didn't even know that their opinions were making my life downright "unlivable."

It reminded me of how I used to experience so many mixed emotions when I'd see women in full burka in Brooklyn: alarm, followed by a certain feminist irk, and finally discomfiture at our cultural kinship. And then it would all turn into one strong emotion—protective rage—when I'd see a group of teenagers laughing and pointing at them.

❋

Every day, more and more, I lost America and America lost me. But I should have been in my honeymoon phase, since I was actually a farily new American. In the autumn of 2001, not long after the towers fell, as luck would have it, my citizenship papers finally went through. That November, I was in a Brooklyn federal courtroom singing, along with a room full of immigrants, the national anthem that I hadn't sung since I was in school.

I remember, on that day, 9/11 leaving the foreground of my mind for the first time. I remember looking around the room and feeling, in spite of myself, some sense of optimism about the future. I remember feeling like I was a part of something. I remember the feeling of my official introduction to the collection of words that would from now on gracefully declare and demarcate my two worlds: Middle Eastern–American. The same hyphen has felt like a dagger that coarsely divides what had once been a symbol of a tragic and hallowed bond.

Today Is a Sunny Day

For years, I have tried to write about the events that occurred on 9/11.

The turning point of my life, I have written many times.

This is taken from the first time I tried, dated 13 September 2001:

There are two red gaping wounds coming out
of a sight she knows all too well, those two tall
towers that always stood higher than the rest, those
boring monoliths she used to complain about
seeing daily, never a fan of seventies architecture.
Jon, her boyfriend, eventually came to her side and
her next sentence was, "Turn on the television,
something is happening." On NY1 she saw the

exact same thing as out of her window—it was as
if they were indistinguishable, what was in front
of her, what was filtered through the television,
the reality of it as cinematic as . . . cinema. On
the news they said many things, but the errors
stand out: the planes were private jets, there was a
third plane somewhere in the NYC skyline about
to come down, the D.C. mall was on fire. It was
all unclear. They took out a disposable camera
and took pictures for reasons they could not
understand, but probably so they could just believe
it was happening. The buildings were sparkling
wildly, covered in a halo of glitter from all the
broken glass.

✱

I applied to grad school the month after 9/11, because I had
to do something with myself.

For an entire semester, every story I workshopped started
out being about something else and ended up being about
9/11.

I don't stand by those stories today, but I somehow envy
their immaturity.

Because what could you do but wedge yourself into the
narrative, until the story was a story of you, and the crime
against the self, *your* self to be specific, and the terrorists had
downed you, the city hurting for you and you alone?

✱

And yet when you try to make sense of all the layers of non-fiction, fiction, with its insistence on order, creeps in to tidy the narrative.

The writer Don DeLillo talks about how in the future, people will insert themselves into the scene: "For the next fifty years, people who were not in the area when the attacks occurred will claim to have been there. In time, some of them will believe it. Others will claim to have lost friends or relatives, although they did not. This is also the counternarrative, a shadow history of false memories and imagined loss." How accurate this turned out to be. On September 12, 2001, I sent an email to a few dozen friends that said, among other things, that "two people I know seem to be of the 'missing.'"

I don't know which two I meant. When I reread the email, I wanted to punch myself. And yet another side of me wanted to break down and mourn for the pressure and sorrow in composing that email. Who knew what chaos fueled that confusion. And then there's DeLillo's counternarrative, that "shadow history of false memories and imagined loss." There is an endless stream of new truths being born, events in flux and therefore never over. How can there be closure on something that we won't allow to close? Who can call the closure when it belongs to no one and everyone?

※

Thanksgiving 2001, a journal entry:

I have become an American citizen. It just so happened my date to be sworn in arrived after my

application had been in the works for a year or so.
It was a good thing, because in September 2001,
my green card expired, and I've been worrying
seriously that all Middle Eastern people would
be put in some internment camp or deported. I
thought it was a good thing to become a citizen—
being a real resident of this country would allow
me the freedom to leave the country (and of course
come back) and I could vote, both blessed luxuries.
So I went through my interviews with the INS,
of which there were a couple. One time, an INS
official, checking my language skills, asked me to
write "today is a sunny day" and I wrote it in a
shaky cursive that didn't even look like my own
handwriting. I answered the official's questions
(*What are the colors of our flag?* to the admittedly
more challenging *What are the duties of Congress?*),
and went to the naturalization ceremony where we
sang the national anthem and pledged allegiance and
some people were crying and laughing and just a
few, like myself, were somewhere between solemn,
stoic, and confused.

Welcome to America. After two decades.

Just three months later, another entry, my first reflection
on being American:

I began taking Amtraks cross-country for months as
a way to avoid planes—9/11 had only heightened
my fear of flying to total paralysis—and recently in

the middle of those multi-day voyages I got to test
out my Americanness while feeling the full force
of my Iranianness. Somewhere up in Rochester or
Buffalo—one of those dreary northern New York
industrial towns—in the middle of the night, the
train stopped and state troopers stormed in like
the bad-looking good guys of a movie. They had
an urgency that woke people up more abruptly
than even the sound of their shoes or the boom
of their voices, which I remember as being eerily
lowered as if to show some consideration but
instead only evoking a creepy sort of ax murderer
murmur. Apparently they had a question in the
form of a demand for all of us, each and every one,
and it involved putting flashlights into our eyes
and uttering it, a cluster of seats at a time: "Please
state the country of your citizenship." I had finally
fallen asleep after hours of the dull sort of alertness
that train travel can inspire in some, and I was
very disoriented when they woke me with their
calculated hullabaloo. I think the whole point was to
catch us off guard, because some people seemed to
pause. I remember at first muttering "Iran," because
I had always known myself as an Iranian citizen;
my whole life I wrote I-R-A-N on the dotted line.
But the minute it fell out of my mouth, I felt like
a person who had thrown herself off a bridge and
only midway decided it was a mistake—I didn't
mean to do that. It wasn't even true! Life was good:
I was an American! I quickly took it back by almost

shouting into the man's face, "America, America, I am an American citizen, yes." The man paused, and we looked at each other with a bit of the swagger of cowboys at a shootout, squint for squint, scowl for scowl. Finally the man walked on and I was free. And I thought that was the first time I did not feel safe as an American, because my Americanness was a hyphenated one and even if I "passed" and others didn't know it, somehow my very own identity could leak out and needlessly betray me.

*

Interviewers and critics have called me a "9/11 author." My first novel, *Sons and Other Flammable Objects*, which I began in 2003 and which was published in 2007, had a bloodred cover featuring the silhouette of a dove flying just over a shadowed New York skyline that prominently featured the World Trade Center. And it's true that 9/11 takes up much of the book—it is both an antagonist and a protagonist. It is what breaks men up and brings them back together.

But the attacks do not actually appear in the novel.

The minutes after do. My protagonist, the quarter-life-crisis-afflicted Xerxes Adam, places a call to his mother to say, "Mother, I am alive," after months of estrangement from his family in Los Angeles, and the hours after—meeting his soon-to-be girlfriend on the rooftop of an East Village apartment complex that they are both residents of, in the evening after, in front of a still-smoking skyline. The months before appear also. The serious squabbles that split people up that can later be seen as petty fights in the dark light of 9/11. And there are the months after: the sense of placelessness for New York City residents, the horror of a routinely stalled subway car, the endless lines at a post office where postal workers donned gloves and masks, a time when people called 911 on planes that looked too big or seemed to fly too low or packages that felt strangely packed with addresses that looked too foreign. It was a time when you had to act normal, where the passing of months could be marked by how many fewer color-copied photos of the missing you saw in the city.

It took my second novel to take me *there*. The impetus for the narrative was to include something few speak or write about, something I didn't have the courage to write about previously: the idea that the end of the story of 9/11 contained in it some small but real sparks of beauty. In an early draft of my second novel, *The Last Illusion*, started in 2009 and finished in 2011, ten years after the event and totally fixated on it—costumed in a sort of magical realist take—I wrote an ending made up of the moments on the street before we got in a car and left the city, chronicling the most surprising thing we saw:

> The whole city was screaming in sirens, police and
> fire trucks and ambulances all at different intervals
> talking over each other, the only sounds, because
> the men and women who were running seemed
> mostly silent.

And there was a strange stillness, a sense that it would get even worse before it got worse.

And as far as you'd run, it felt like you were still close.

And suddenly men and women covered in a white dust were running, men and women shouting and screaming. They were wearing parts of buildings, Zal realized, they were wrapped in the building's carnage. The buildings had died on them and they had somehow still lived.

And Zal ran with them, fast, and he noticed a few were not just silent but shouting and not crying but laughing. One man was pumping his fists in the air yelling, We made it! And another woman was crying and grinning at the same time, hands in prayer, thanking something in the sky.

They made Zal stop dead in his tracks, against the runners. He stopped, mesmerized by their faces, the brief moment of joy in all that world-ending clamour.

He watched the city move in its frantic motion, away from the end of the island, away from its end, toward itself, toward its heart. And he moved with it, with them, and counted what smiles he saw among the many tears and looks of shock and defeat.

The city was going to be plastered with the smiling faces of their family, friends, and neighbors for months. That was all that was going to be left of those unlucky ones, so frozen in their smiles.

❋

The ending to this novel actually came from a journal entry scribble, just a frantic note—*saw people smiling?!*—that had an attached parenthetical halfway down the page: *detail you might want to leave out.* It took me a decade to realize that the only truths worth anything in the end were those very details that, in resisting narrative, told the real story.

The Forever Refugee

When news of Donald Trump's executive order, the Muslim ban, broke, I had just started a new semester of adjunct teaching at Columbia University. I was relieved to put my phone on silent, mentally shelve the news, and face a new classroom. I was walking with a cane—I'd had late-stage Lyme disease for years—and I wondered which joke to lead with first: something that would disarm them about my illness, or something about how their professor might be in an internment camp before their finals. I did neither. I dreaded the end of class, when I'd have to look at my phone again—wondering which part of my identity would clash with what fresh news update: partially disabled, chronically ill, Iranian, American, artist, academic, journalist, woman.

I've been teaching in America since 2003. It's in my

blood; my father has been an adjunct professor in California since the early 1980s. Decades later I am someone who, like my father, sees the academy as home.

By Friday of that week, a day I spent largely between browsers on my computer—rumor had it that Donald Trump was maybe minutes, maybe seconds away, from signing the Muslim ban, around 4:30 p.m.—I was making syllabi for two other classes I taught at Bard College. Three thousand miles away, my father was doing the same thing.

The rest of that night for me was not unlike many I've had since 9/11. I spent it reading news articles, crying, and wondering: What is going to happen to this country? What will they do to my other country? You can be a refugee once, I've always thought, but how to be one twice?

As a child, I accepted that we were different, but I reminded myself that that was the mission of America, "the land of immigrants," a haven for those who had lost their homelands. I wanted to write books because reading and writing were all we had when we fled from Iran to Turkey through Europe and eventually to the United States. My first memories are of air raids, sirens, long bus rides, the anguish of my parents, the revolving temporary homes, from Swiss convent to Skid Row motel, but also of books. Paper and pen and books that my parents bought here and there replaced the toys I had in Iran.

The paper and pens are still my life now. It's the life I teach my students. It's the life I participate in socially. I believe in stories, I believe in art, I believe in culture. I believe these are the things we have in common.

It took September 11 to teach me that many would find

my identity an impossibility, that my Iranian and American sides represented incompatibility at best.

Before 9/11, I had laughed at the terms *naturalized* and *resident alien*. But it wasn't because I didn't see the bigotry. I knew in my first few years of America in the 1980s that we were hated, every time someone asked me where I was from—this was the era of "Nuke Iran" bumper stickers, and I now own a button from that time period that features a different four-letter word before the country where I was born. But it took 9/11 to make me realize I was culturally Muslim and proud, and that in spite of no practice, I would forever be part of the story of Islamophobia.

I thought back on those experiences when hearing from and reading about those affected by Trump's executive order. I was safe, with the semester fully under way and in my element, among students and colleagues. I've always felt safest on college campuses, where the promise of American freedom felt most realized to me. As a child, I was obsessed with the concept of freedom of expression, not to mention education's potential as a great equalizer. In school, I believed I could exist alongside the rich and share access to their opportunities, study with mentors who could help me reach those dreams. Just the potential was meaningful. Was it a bubble? A dream? Our history books were full of examples of those like me, immigrants who had fled religious persecution or whose ancestors share that story—who had made their dreams reality.

I talked to many friends about what might happen after the Muslim ban, and this was the one thing I kept coming back to: I hoped I wouldn't have to leave mid-semester. There were rumors that naturalized citizens might be targeted next.

The mention of "Iran" on my passport has always caused me problems—I was detained and questioned relentlessly for many hours in Tel Aviv this past summer on a work trip, used to joke for hours with other brown people and the Irish in our "special lines" at Heathrow, and I have many more stories of international and domestic travel mishaps thanks to my name and country of origin. I've accepted that. But when I imagined being pried away from my life here, what guts me most is the idea of the end of my service here, my separation from what has given meaning to my life. College campuses are the only homes my father and I have ever had; they are the places that bridge our hyphenated identities.

Some people would say that my father and I are both successes, and they applaud us for achieving the American Dream. But when we have a president who boasts of reading no books, of not using computers, who has a deep suspicion of media, who ran a fraudulent university, what hope is there for the life of the mind? Given that this kind of life is already undervalued economically in this country, that question is less theoretical than it sounds. We couldn't afford to leave, in all of the senses of *afford*. And now add to it that *our actual lives* might be rendered valueless by our own country's government.

On election day, my mother wrote me: "I know you are disappointed, frustrated and sad, as most of us are today. Today I felt exactly the same way that I felt 37 years ago when our country went through revolution and we had to leave the country that we loved and grew up in. We survived and started all over again here and today we have two wonderful, successful kids and a place called home again. That was a change for life, but this is not! This change is only for 4 years or maybe 8 years. So keep having hope, work hard and stay positive because this does not last forever."

I thought of how after hours of trying to console my distraught college freshmen last semester, I landed on, *We can do this. My family and I did it before*, I said, *and if it comes to that, you can do this, too.* The problem is that I can't tell them with certainty what *this* is.

A Muslim-American
in Indonesia

In December 2015, I was slated to go back to the country of my birth: Iran. Nearly a year before, an editor at *Condé Nast Traveler* had reached out to me, wondering if I might be interested in being sent to Iran. She did not, of course, realize that this would be my first trip back to the country since I was three, nor that there would be substantial complications given that I was a dual citizen. Iran refuses to recognize my US citizenship. After a new batch of imprisonment of Iranian dual citizens, the trip was canceled. Jason Rezaian, the Iranian-American journalist who had been imprisoned for eighteen months in Evin Prison, was released just weeks after my planned trip. I remember feeling gutted by this loss—a trip where I'd explore Tehran, Shiraz, and Isfahan. It felt important for me to go back to a place I did not know, but still called *home*.

The closest I'd been to Iran since I left was when I flew to Australia for various book festivals in the spring of 2015. My Emirates flight stopover was in Dubai, and I calculated that I was only 750 miles from my birthplace. As we approached the night skyline of Dubai, I looked down at the same sky-view glitter of my refugee home Los Angeles, but with the notable Burj gleaming shamelessly like a sword. My many hours there on both legs of the flight were relatively fruitless. I searched the faces of those I saw, as I knew Dubai had a substantial Iranian population, but that effort did not yield much. More than that, I was in awe of the fact that I was in a region where the majority of people were somewhat like me—Middle Eastern, of a Muslim culture. But I was hard-pressed to see that in a hub like Dubai International. As I bought cartons of Gauloises at the duty-free shop, I marveled at the East Asians, Europeans, and even Americans around me. I was not going to get much of a cultural experience here.

What I did not realize was that during the flight from Dubai to Perth, I'd fly over Iranian airspace. I wouldn't have known this if not for the flight-tracker monitor in front of me—but there it was, as if Iran were no big deal, as if revolution or not, it was a country that existed, that you could go to, that you could just casually fly over. I watched those very cities that I was planning to visit in December announce themselves underneath me in a flash: Tehran, Shiraz, Isfahan, plus Qom and Mashhad. Outside the window it was just before dusk, and all you could see was the hazy brown of mountain upon mountain. For a second I felt like my longing could fill the plane. And after a couple of weeks of touring through Australia, what I looked forward to most was the ride back in Iranian airspace. This time I was not so lucky as to have a window seat, and I nearly flattened the South Asian grandmother next to me as I leaned into the window. *Sorry, it's Iran, I was born there, and I haven't been back,* I said to her. She didn't seem to understand, as my body weight was up against her. I pulled back. I muttered to her, but really to myself, *I'm going to go back one day soon.*

I haven't yet. But half a year later, I found myself on another long international flight, this time on Cathay Pacific via Hong Kong to Jakarta, for more book festivals. It was on the final leg after Hong Kong—a city I'd been excited to visit my whole life—when a realization hit me: my trip to Jakarta would be the first time I would be in a Muslim country since Iran. I imagined what this could mean: veils, prayers, Korans, beads, all the paraphernalia of a childhood I had mostly missed. On this book festival circuit, I would be largely in Ubud, Bali, but I'd agreed to do satellite programs in Jakarta and Semarang, and my affiliates there had arranged for me to speak at several colleges. I had no idea what to expect, but I knew this experience was going to be significant.

Semarang was the first proper city I visited, and I had little idea of it, other than we'd be there for a couple of days, that I'd speak to two colleges, and then we'd be off to Bali, where I was staying at a very upscale resort and there would be so many parties and great food and good writer friends. When we landed on the Garuda flight from Jakarta, I was taken immediately with the colorful prints of the clothes nearly everyone wore, matched even more brilliantly with headscarves. I realized I was probably the only person who could call Islam her culture who was bareheaded, not to mention tattooed, in a tank top, wearing garish lipstick as if dressed for an American spring break. I wondered if they could tell; if they could, they were too polite, or perhaps too disapproving, to look. Maybe I was invisible, maybe in a good way.

At the hotel, as tired as I was, I could not pry myself from the window. Semarang is the largest city in the province of Central Java and looked not unlike the Los Angeles of my eighties youth—the sky a murky yellow-gray, smog and haze competing for complete saturation. But if you could spot a handful of bikers on highways there, here nearly everyone was on a motorcycle. And it wasn't those Vespas like in Rome. These were cheap old motorbikes, and drivers rode them with companions and often a child or two or even three. This was a land with bigger issues than safety, and you got the feeling these cyclists were not on joyrides, but commuting urgently to work or home.

I asked my handler why the motorbikes were so popular, and she blinked at me as if I were kidding, snapping, *Of course they are cheaper than cars.* I watched with admiration as they zigzagged with little attention to lanes, ran red lights, made spontaneous U-turns, and honked mercilessly. The chaos had a logic to it. Your attention serves as the substitute for rules. Hypervigilance gets built in as a survival technique, and you ease into it. If I had had more days there, I would have likely been converted as a rider myself.

But I had work to do. I was to deliver two talks, and I was dreading them. It took arriving at the first destination to understand just how challenging that experience would be. The representative from the US embassy seemed very relaxed about my duties and assured me that it would be the sort of talk I was used to, no preparation necessary. *Had they read my books?* I wondered. *Probably not*, she said, but not to worry, it would be easy. On my crumpled schedule, the program publicist had written that the talk was to be "a discussion with acclaimed author and *New York Times* contributor Porochista Khakpour, exploring her life, background, and work as a woman of Iranian descent with Muslim lineage. How has her identity contributed to her personal journey and literary career? And what place does the concept of America, and the 9/11 WTC bombings have in her work?"

Easy enough, everyone seemed to say. But when I arrived at Walisongo State Islamic University, a public Muslim college, I saw a giant orange banner across a stage: "American Corner Talkshow: Being a Minority with Porochista Khakpour." I immediately felt a bit light-headed—those wild words and their promise, plus the overpowering heat. It was ninety degrees in Semarang. The large room was full of electric fans, and buzzing with what seemed like hundreds of young people. It seemed unendurable to me. I tried to focus on something, anything, but everything was a wave of color and heat and sound. The headscarves stood out—also the smiles. There was genuine excitement among them for . . . me. They led me "backstage," which was a faculty lounge of sorts, where a lavish spread had been prepared for me—fruit, nuts, cookies, tea. Professors greeted me with huge smiles and handshakes. I started to hear "Muslim author" a lot.

It is so good to hear a Muslim author from America, an administrator kept saying.

I finally had to say something. *I'm not—well, I don't practice Islam. I am of a Muslim culture, but I don't* . . . I had absently pointed to my head, but I also meant to point at my tattoos, my loud lipstick, my drinking, my history of drugging, my singleness, my lack of praying—all of it.

Everyone just smiled and nodded, and moments later I was introduced by the US embassy and handed a microphone. I began to ramble about my experience as an immigrant who had become an American finally in 2001 and then an Iranian-American author in 2007, hoping they would catch a word or two at most. But they were all watching and nodding, attentive. When the question-and-answer period came around—an hour was allotted for it—I imagined that since my book had not been taught, there would be no questions.

There were dozens and dozens.

How does it feel being Iranian in the United States today?

How do Americans consider Muslims?

If I move to America, can I be respected as Muslim?

There was not a light question in the mix. I rambled my way through them and somehow the program concluded to applause. Then I became aware of another Indonesian tradition—photos. Everyone wanted selfies with me. A full half hour, I realized, had been allotted for the taking of photos. By the end of my day there, I had a few hundred more Instagram friends.

What followed was a polite and charming seafood dinner with journalists and academics at a local restaurant, and I found myself telling various people I knew I'd never see again that I would be back and that I would love to stay in touch. Then we were back at the hotel, and my handlers informed me that tomorrow I'd be doing the same thing again. Different school, same drill.

They did not tell me that this time it was a Christian school, Soegijapranata Catholic University, in a far wealthier part of town. I was immediately greeted by hordes of faculty, who handed me elaborate snack boxes and lots of tea. The US embassy rep had warned me that I'd have another banner, so I blinked less when I saw the same giant banner, this time in purple with similar words: "A General Lecture on Multicultural America: Being a Minority by Porochista Khakpour." This time, instead of a hot, crowded assembly room, I was on a modern amphitheater stage. There were no headscarves in the audience, but you could easily see a difference in income level in the way the students were dressed.

There were the same questions, but this time about being Christian. It occurred to me that these students were the minority, Christians in a Muslim-majority country.

I tried my best, I felt inadequate, selfies upon selfies upon selfies, and that was that.

When we left Semarang for the airport the next day—bound for Bali, where the actual main event, the Ubud Writers and Readers Festival, would take place—I found myself thinking about that city. On the cab ride to the airport, the cabdriver honked and honked.

No one gets upset? I asked my handler.

She looked confused. *Why?*

The honking, I said. *In America, it's rude or at least aggressive.*

She seemed surprised. *It's courtesy and respect here. They don't want you to crash.*

Of course, I thought.

And, of course, Bali was a dream. I stayed at a luxury hotel in the monkey jungle, had my first encounter with a proper Olympic-size infinity pool, reveled in a festival that was as exhilarating as it was glamorous—there were multiple festivities at the royal palace—but it was not until my final days of satellite events, this time back in Jakarta, that I felt like I was in Indonesia again.

*

I would not have guessed that Jakarta, perhaps especially after the unexpected joys of Semarang, would become one of my favorite cities on earth. We had only a few days in this coastal city, at the mouth of the Ciliwung on Jakarta Bay, on the world's most populous island. Everyone, including Indonesians, had warnings for me about Jakarta—it was too dirty, too crowded, too loud, too ugly. There seemed to be little love for it. *Just look at our sky*, a taxi driver said, and indeed there was Semarang's—and my eighties L.A.'s—gray-yellow backdrop, though even more gray, in a way that made all the highway flora, amply planted, look almost surreal in their pinks and purples against the bleak newsprint tones of concrete and sky. *Look at our traffic*, he said later, much later, as it took us some hours to get to my hotel. Many echoed the expression, telling me it was a good reason to not explore much.

Still, I explored. Our base, the Artotel Thamrin, was a hip boutique hotel. Located in the city center, the hotel had collaborated with eight emerging visual artists, whose work was on display in each hall and room. The effect made it look like an East Berlin hostel, a bit careless, a bit punk, but also very calculated in its youthfulness. I walked around the city center, poking in and out of stores, malls, and gem shops. The days

revolved around food: nonstop nasi goreng, a fried-rice deli-
cacy with skewered meats, satay, fried fish and fish dumplings.
My favorite treat was a street food, martabak, which my team
seemed especially excited to introduce me to. We sat at night
with beers and heavy cartons full of the sweet treat, a folded
pancake filled with Toblerone and butter that seemed nearly
impossible to consume in the overwhelming, viscous heat of
the tropical monsoon night. Everything became drenched in
sweat. Jakartans explained to me that they found it shocking
that Americans bathe only once a day—not only do they
bathe multiple times but they wash their clothes daily, too.

The city used to be known as Koningin van het Oosten
(Queen of the East) during its colonial period, but today it
was the Big Durian (after the horrifically odored fruit that
I had learned to avoid that trip), like the Big Apple. And it
had qualities similar to New York's. It was manic and urgent
and all about work and the impossibility of work. It was a
wonderful mess. All around, a diversity of architectural styles
revealed themselves—from my modern base to Malay, Java-
nese, Arabic, Chinese, and Dutch influences, the Old Town
melted into the New with little hesitation. This place felt like
a real melting pot.

I found myself wondering if my hometown, Tehran,
would feel like this, a question I could not answer.

Jakarta was, of course, a major Muslim capital too, with
the population at over 85 percent Muslim, the rest Protestant,
Catholic, Buddhist, and Hindu mainly. I heard the *azan*, the
Muslim call to prayer, over the loudspeakers in the city, and
this turned out to be one of the most important experiences
of my life.

My first memories from Iran were not happy ones—air raids, bomb sirens, panic and revolution and war, as I was born into the Iranian Revolution and then the Iran-Iraq War. One of the memories I also have of that era is looking out the window facing my crib and seeing men wailing on rooftops in prayer. I remember the visual scared me, because it was tied to change, which my parents recognized to be threatening. It was something I would not understand as part of my culture for many years.

In Jakarta, I woke to the sound of the prayer, and my days were punctuated by the sound. At a dinner with journalists, some almost apologetically mentioned to me that the city had been trying for years to get mosques to lower the volume, but it was delicate, as the effort could be interpreted as disrespectful to Muslims.

You don't want to offend Muslims, a journalist said to me in total earnestness, a sentence I could never have imagined in America.

I found the sound so beautiful. I found myself recording the prayers, over and over, and treasuring this folder on my laptop devoted to the calls of Muslim devotion in Jakarta. I found myself trying to mouth the words one morning.

The other event there that tied me to this special city was the satellite program's impromptu affiliation with a local poetry group, which had asked for us to make guest appearances at their local slam night on the rooftop of the Artotel I was staying in. My traveling companion, an editor, and I reluctantly obliged—neither of us were poets—and imagined we'd sit in the audience, a bit clueless, as we were warned the event would not be in English.

But that night became a significant night: again so overbearingly hot and humid that the air burst into monsoon downpour and the deck of the roof turned into a covered vestibule for us, and a shelter of many special hours. The members of the group were young Jakartans who didn't look all that different from my liberal arts college students in New York. Many of them pointed out to us that they were part of LGBTQIA organizations in town. They were all excited that we lived in New York and wanted badly to speak about it with us. They read all sorts of things, some in English even, perhaps to humor us—Sylvia Plath's "Daddy" was rendered like horror theater by a young gay man, and then a Bukowski poem I'd never read was uttered in a throaty whisper by a beautiful young woman in a tiny black dress and sky-high heels. They got it, these Jakartans, and I was reminded of my first slams in New York City in the nineties—it was so vulnerable, so powerful, so naked, so sheltering.

They asked me to share something. Just the summer before, I had begun writing poems, with no intention of sharing them at all. I dove into my laptop and found a draft of a rough poem. They applauded me not like some famous author who was doing a reading for them, but as a peer. It was a beautiful feeling, and I felt impossibly young and new and excited about words again in a way I hadn't for many years.

When I got back to America I thought of this group, Malam Puisi. We emailed and tried to arrange for me to Skype into their session, as their night would be my day. All of Indonesia stayed with me. I stayed in touch with my handlers, I played the Muslim prayers over and over, I dreamed of the dirty skies and the colorful prints and the neon flora that fought its dismalness at every step. I felt haunted by its importance to me, how oddly I felt I belonged there, too, in a country where for once I was culturally part of a majority.

The morning I left Jakarta, the sky was a burnt pink. *The fires*, my taxi driver said, *don't you know?* I didn't. I came to learn about it: palm oil and paper pulp companies illegally set fire to forests to clear land to plant more trees, justifying the practice because it was cheap and fast. This was an annual problem, and this time it had resulted in 8,063 square miles of forests and other land burned and twenty-one deaths. More than half a million people were sickened with respiratory problems, and the country faced $9 billion in economic losses, for everything from damaged crops to hundreds of canceled flights. He told me I was lucky to be leaving, and I remember feeling a worry for Indonesia.

Ten days after my last night there, the world fell into grief and panic over the Paris attacks, and Muslims became suspect again, not that they ever weren't. I became a news junkie again. On social media, I begged for tolerance for Muslims, often thinking of how I had answered the questions of those young Muslim students:

How does it feel being Iranian in the US today?
It feels mostly okay. It has been a long road. Americans in the eighties were not so tolerant, but I have hope for our future. . . .

How do Americans consider Muslims?
It took some time after 9/11, of course, but I would say the Americans I closely associate with are very tolerant and generally quite curious about Muslims, at least in the big cities. . . .

If I move to America, can I be respected as Muslim?
I personally believe so, though it may take some patience and educating on your end. . . .

But I worried about whether my answers were accurate. New York felt poised for another attack, and I suffered insomnia online late at night, inhaling news and battling bigots.

It was late one night, too late my time, that I saw the hashtag #PrayforJakarta pop up from my poetry group friends on Twitter. Right next to the Artotel, there had been an explosion outside a Starbucks and then another at a police station. At least eight people—four attackers and four civilians—were killed, and twenty-three others were injured. ISIS claimed responsibility within hours.

I stayed with my Malam Puisi friends on Twitter as they remained indoors. All I could think of were their performances of Plath and Bukowski, their open spirits, how they had brought us into their world so effortlessly, how they had expected we'd stay in touch.

Back and forth we wrote, and their final words before I went to bed were *We're fine. We're not afraid. Thank you for your prayer. Hugs.*

Hugs to you, back in my favorite city, I tweeted to them.

I've been trying to write about that magical night of poetry on the rooftop of the hotel during the rains.

This is my story for them.

The Father of Iran's Nuclear Weapons Program

1

On the day that my second novel, *The Last Illusion*, was published, six world powers met in Vienna to attempt to begin the end of decade-long talks about Iran's nuclear capabilities.

In 2007, my first novel's pub date coincided with then Iranian president Mahmoud Ahmadinejad's visit to New York.

And so I would like to say that my books inspire peaks in the Iran news cycle, but then I remind myself: Has there been a time in almost four decades when Iran was *not* in the news?

Still, December 4, 2014, matters, and it's not because of my book. Iran's foreign minister has claimed that the seven nations who are meeting—Iran, the United States, France, Germany, Britain, China, and Russia—are in "50 to 60 percent agreement" on a nuclear deal. But the United States has stated that the accords need 100 percent agreement on both sides. The West suspects that Iran may be seeking nuclear weapons capability and thus has deployed sanctions and the threat of more sanctions against Iran. Meanwhile, Iran maintains that its program is peaceful, and that it needs substantial uranium-enrichment capacities to make low-enriched reactor fuel.

By the self-imposed July 20, 2015, deadline for agreement, Iran and the West need to come to a resolution. Or the usual "or else" will prevail, particularly ominous-sounding when referring to Iran. Iranian clerics enjoy the doomsday mystique a bit: "Our negotiators should not accept any coercive words from the other party," Supreme Leader Ali Khamenei told Iranian nuclear scientists during Iran's National Day of Nuclear Technology. "The country's nuclear achievements can't be stopped." Meanwhile, the average Iranian wants relief from sanctions that have crippled the already crippled Iranian economy. Some limited relief has been offered since January, since minor nuclear activities were seemingly halted.

In Iran, the country's nuclear weapons program has been a source of something like pride—for hard-liners and moderates alike. I myself am the daughter of an Iranian nuclear scientist (albeit a theoretical physicist, with a PhD from MIT), and many members of my family have been in some way involved with the Atomic Energy Organization of Iran (AEOI). My parents met each other there. Most significantly, my great-uncle, whom I'd been quite close to since childhood, is known as the father of Iran's nuclear weapons program in the Western press.

Akbar Etemad was the deputy prime minister under the Shah in the 1970s and also head of the AEOI between 1974 and 1978—important years in Iranian history, just before the revolution would alter Iranian history unlike anything else. He has said that even under the Shah, nuclear weapons were a priority of the Iranian government—a priority the United States was favorably disposed toward. Americans were initially supportive, he recalls, "because they thought they were going to be a partner of Iran in the application of nuclear technology. . . . I had the impression that the Americans wanted to impose their views on Iran, and I refused to deal with them. We were discussing for four years the terms of the bilateral agreement and we never came to a conclusion."

He goes on: "The Shah had the idea at the time that he's strong enough in the region and he can defend our interests in the region, [and] he didn't want nuclear weapons. But he told me that if this changes, 'We have to go for nuclear.' He had that in mind. My mission was to go for all the technologies imaginable in the field of nuclear technology."

My great-uncle, who now lives in exile in Paris, where he fled for political asylum and has stayed following the revolution, has also said: "I think Iran has the right to do the research that they are doing and I don't see why the Western countries impose sanctions against Iran. They pressure Iran. Why didn't they do it with India, Pakistan, and Israel?"

These are quotes I've found on the Internet. I don't talk to my great-uncle anymore, but I do read about him from afar—sometimes with some confusion, sometimes with pride. Our rift is rooted in an episode where I'd heard secondhand that he'd told another relative he thought my first novel, *Sons and Other Flammable Objects*, portrayed Iranians too negatively. That felt especially hurtful because, of all my relatives, he was the one who had seemed to understand me the most.

I remember visiting him in London when I was on my junior year abroad at Oxford, and journeying from pub to pub with him late into the night. He always had the air of a mischievous teenager. He was the one relative who approved of my magenta-streaked hair and all my other rebellions, and who did not blink an eye when he caught me smoking. I missed him, but I didn't know where to start with him again. *The Last Illusion* would not be where to start, though its basis lies in a particularly treasured myth, one that sits deep in the psyche of Iranians.

2

A question that comes up sometimes in different forms, in interviews, at signings, and occasionally from friends and associates is this: *Are you proud to be Iranian?* Or: *Aren't you proud to be Iranian?*

They do not say Iranian-American or, as a book reviewer recently put it, American-Iranian. My Americanness could not possibly be problematic.

I say yes and try not to overthink it. I imagine a young stranger in Iran counting on my pride—though in reality he would probably regard my pride with a healthy helping of skepticism. *Aren't you proud to be an American?*

3

The time I came second-closest to going to Iran was when I booked a ticket several years ago—the fruits of a drunken all-nighter with a famous war correspondent during which we graphed and charted, through many martinis, a plot to sneak me in and out of Iran on a speedboat from Bahrain. At this point, Evin Prison in Tehran was making the Iranian government some money from the bails of imprisoned American scholars, journalists, and wayward hikers. So the illicit movements we plotted actually sounded prudent.

My father is the only member of our family who has been back—in 2008, months after he read my first novel, in which a father books a ticket to go back to Iran for the first time. My father did that exactly—in his words, "to show it wasn't a big deal." He had a great time, he said, but retains no record of it. He had an old camera that used film. He dropped it at LAX on his way home, and the photos were destroyed.

My connection to life in Iran is about as strong as any American's connection to life in Iran. It has come largely from the news.

But in recent years I've corresponded with more and more Iranians. Iranians have connected with me on social media, with proxy servers now so advanced that there are all sorts of back-alley ways to enter the Internet.

A few weeks ago, a new Facebook follower—let's call her Hyacinth—began liking a lot of posts pertaining to my new book and books in general. She wrote me a message:

I live in Urmia, West Azerbaijan, Iran, and as I
was born in wartime between Iran and Iraq, I
write stories for war children and interested in war
literature, but unfortunately because of sanctions, no
new books are available here, and what I have are
old classics, and nothing more.

Hyacinth seemed to want me to send her instructional
material and literature. It was heartbreaking to receive this
from a beautiful stranger who beamed at me in a photo in
which she wore a loose headscarf and sunglasses, whose page
was mainly nature shots and inspirational quotes, writing me
wanting to know more about books.

I tried to get additional information from her—the sanctions issue interested me. She wrote back:

Well, i really don't know exactly why this happened,
because i was student out side the country and
when i came back original books were not much
available, and when i asked bookstores, they told
me because of all sanctions publications are not
interested to import their books, though years a
go just classics and some moderns were available,
but not any new novels, and one point is if we
can find any original book here, it's very very
expensive, for example I bought Kafka's America
about 550,000 rial [$21.50 USD] which is not
easy for every student to get it. so many students
have to find the books or text by internet and make

copy of them. another problem is we don't have access to international banks and international credit cards, so we can not by the books online, though i am not talking about rich people, because they have everything, money talks you know!

I googled "Iran + sanctions + books" but couldn't find much. I didn't know what it was like to live in a culture in which someone can be *that* hungry for books, where the possession of books signifies freedom. I couldn't believe it, and I am a writer, someone who *should* believe in that.

It forced me to eye my many shelves of books with a strange distance, which might have actually been a newfound intimacy. And especially as the publication date of my novel neared, I tried to hold my novel the way I imagined Hyacinth would. With some baseline reverence.

4

The Persian Book of Kings, or the Shahnameh, is what the major story line of my second novel is based on. The Book of Kings is a phone book–size magnum opus made up of fifty thousand couplets, the national epic of Iran written by the poet Ferdowsi in the tenth century. It's a mix of historic and mythic annals from ancient pre-Islamic Persia up until the Arab conquests of AD 651. Almost every Iranian I've ever met can recite portions or at least recall some of the stories contained in it. For us, it is a cross between *The Canterbury Tales*, the *Odyssey*, and the Old Testament.

My father used to read me stories from it before I went to bed as a child. My favorite was the story of Zal, an albino born to the royal family who was cast off into the woods because of his unusual appearance. There he was raised by the giant mythical bird of Persian legend, the Simorgh, before eventually returning to his kingdom as a great warrior.

This, not a nuclear program, is the real pride of Iran. I know my great-uncle would agree.

5

A few weeks ago, my friend the Iranian-American journalist and pundit Hooman Majd tweeted a link in Farsi at me plus "Very cool—for Iranians inside Iran . . . congrats!" The link led to what I guessed was a government site, as my Farsi has lapsed quite a bit in recent years. I didn't see an English option at first, and so I stumbled through it until I gave up and sent it to my father, who emailed back: "Porochista e Azizam, Such a wonderful thing! I cannot be any happier. I had heard about this virtual embassy thing, but I never knew about their website. Thanks so much to Hooman Majd for this." I looked again, and this time saw and hit the English button. Indeed, *Virtual Embassy*, and there I was on the list of "Prominent Iranian-Americans."

I was proud. It's a conflicted pride, of course—Rouhani and Khamenei's Iran is not the Iran I was born in and not the

Iran I am willing to live in. But recognition for the first time from my native home felt like an accomplishment.

"Wow. Well, I'm honored!" I tweeted back to Hooman. And I am.

I tried to write back to Hyacinth, to ask what I could do and what sort of materials and texts she wanted, but her profile was gone. I was frantic trying to remember what she wanted. I recalled only the last post of hers that I saw: "People who shine from within don't need the spotlight," written in a treacly Hallmark cursive.

There might be beauty in her disappearance. I try to find her and then instead make the inevitable post announcing that it's my book's publication date, and the spotlight suddenly feels like I'm under police lights, and my head is thousands and thousands of miles away, on the decisions of those who represent countries instead of countrymen. I want to log off once and for all, too, and find Hyacinth's shine, that elusive contentment, that indeed incandescent pride, that comes from making peace embracing the different sides of yourself completely.

How to Write
Iranian America

Because the machine will try to grind you into dust anyway,
whether or not we speak.

—Audre Lorde

1

Begin by writing about anything else. Go to the public library in your Los Angeles suburb and ask for *all the great books people in New York City read, please.* Wonder if the reference librarian knows a living writer, and ask her what would a living writer read—*and an American one, please.* When she realizes you are in your single digits and asks, *Where are your parents, young lady?* don't answer and demand Shakespeare and take

186

that big book home and cry because you can't understand it. Tomorrow, go back to reading the dictionary a letter at a time and cry because you can't learn the words. Ask your father if you will cry daily for the rest of your life and remember his answer decades later: *When you are older, you will care less about things.* Pray to a god you still believe in that you will once more avoid ESL with all its teachers who look to you with the shine of love but the stench of pity: *refugee, resident alien, political asylum seeker, immigrant, foreigner*—the words you know that you don't want to know.

Write because it's something to do, something you parents will let you do because it looks like homework. Write because one place to live is in your head and it's not broken yet; write because it's something to drown out the sound of your parents fighting deep into the night. When the second-grade teacher—the teacher your father calls an alcoholic—tells you that you will be an author one day and suggests you look at *The Market Guide for Young Writers*, step right up and call yourself a Young Writer. Decide to really write and write about anything but Iranian America. *Ghosts. Victorian girls, maybe ones with tough names. Easter bunnies that are homicidal* (you might have ripped off *Bunnicula*). *Candy. White girls. More white girls.* (Even then you understood sales.) Worry about the fact that your family won't be able to afford a computer and worry about how your fingers get stuck in between the keys of a yellow typewriter your father brought back from Iran, and learn that the only way for your brain not to spiral in worry is to write.

Worry about how you, Young Writer, will ever get to New York City, until you do. Get a scholarship to a fancy college with writers and *writing workshops*, a thing you've never heard of, full of other students told they'd be an author one day. Ignore the dorm politics and the suitemates who tell you their dads paid for you to be there, and write, write. *Los Angeles. The devil. Literary theory. Art. The East Village. White men. And more white men.* Become known as a writer there, a writer who doesn't write about identity. No identity for you, you tell yourself, you tell them. Wear black and big glasses and smoke cigarettes, because you are a New York Young Writer and that can be anyone. When your favorite professor senior year fails your paper on modernism that you've worked on for weeks, when she tells you that she can tell English is your second language, when she tells you maybe writing is not for you, that maybe you need to go into a field like those new *Iranian Studies fields*—you keep imagining these *fields* like those villages of your homeland they label "third world"—go to your dorm and expect to cry but don't. Chain-smoke a pack of cigarettes and never forget her words and commit yourself to writing more, writing more about anything else.

Years later, attend another prestigious college for graduate school, and spend long hours with a famous writer as your professor and adviser who tells you to forget that other professor, that you are a writer, that you can do this. Hold on to her words and almost miss it when she says, *But why don't you write what you know?* Thank her as you always do and hope she doesn't see your tears. Keep turning in stories about anything else. *Math. Chaos theory. Rape.* (The time you were raped but in a sci-fi premise; the time you were raped in a fantasy premise; the time you were raped as something they call metafiction.) *Dogs. Suicidal people. Suicidal people with dogs.*

9/11—although writing about it makes you worry you are getting close to yourself, too close to what you know, which gets a little too close to writing what you know, but keep reminding them that it was because you were a New Yorker, not because you were a Middle Easterner, that you felt the trauma; keep reminding them the hijackers were not Iranian. When they tell you they don't know what you are anyway, don't say a word, just keep working harder and tell yourself you will get the fellowship for another year. Get the fellowship and avoid all their eyes.

When your adviser suggests you work on a novel—that you are, after all, a novelist—hear *novel* like a curse: an arranged marriage and a death sentence, all that unknown potential for devotion to writing anything else.

2

Suddenly you can't write about anything else. Sit in your first apartment without a roommate and realize you have nothing else to write about for the span of a novel. Hate yourself and it, and then go ahead and write it, you're Iranian America, because no one else will see it. This is your first real novel, so what do you know? You are a fellow at a famous university in Baltimore that doesn't pay you enough to teach, so you add on being a hostess at a bistro where the parents of your students go, sometimes with the tenured professors of your department, who pretend they don't see you as they kiss and hug the owner, who sexually harasses you every day. Why would a word you write matter?

Quit smoking, start smoking, quit again, start again.

And watch it come out, more and more in every draft: anger with your parents, frustration with your blood, anxieties surrounding the somehow still-new land—all that is Iranian America. Let your truth come out hard and fast and untranslatable because no one else will see it anyway.

3

They see it. Four years later, it is your first novel and it is published and you are *Miss Literary Iranian America*, a friend jokes. *First Iranian-American novelist*, a journalist mistakenly writes, while another calls your debut novel the first work that is entirely Iranian-American, all diaspora, which gets closer to the truth but not close enough. Who can even tally who they ignored before you? When they ask you to represent the Iranian diaspora in Los Angeles, start by explaining you grew up a half hour and many realities away from Tehrangeles, that you were raised in a tiny apartment in the low-income district of a small suburb, with no other Iranians nearby.

When they ask you to do it anyway, go through with it. Regret quitting smoking. Try to speak of other things. *But what about Iranian-Americans?* they always go, and a friend who is tired of your sighs tells you, *Look, you did that to yourself; it's all in your novel.* Say *fair enough* and start smoking again.

Around Persian New Year, months after your first novel comes out, start to run out of money again. Old problem, but maybe now a new solution, you think. Ask friends if they know someone at the venerable paper where they gave you a very good review of your debut novel. Pitch a piece on Iranians celebrating Persian New Year. Your angle: being Iranian in a bad time to be Iranian. Think to yourself, *When was there ever a good time to be Iranian here?* and pitch it anyway. Hear nothing back and tell yourself you and your Iranian America are not yet worthy of that newspaper.

Be more shocked than gracious a few months later, when, out of nowhere, an editor at another section of that very paper writes you and mentions he is a fan of your work and would you like to contribute an essay to this author series on summer. You can't believe it—this editor has acknowledged your novel and yet is not asking you to write a particular thing about Iranian America. But when you sit down to write, surprise yourself: what you write is about your mother and you, so it's about Iranian America. Feel slightly defeated— *writing what I know was never my thing*, you know you used to whisper—but a part of you anticipates they will want this and they do.

Behold the awe of everyone around you, behold your own awe: you are in your dream paper, an essayist. Editors who never heard of you or your novel start asking for your essays about Iranian America. Soon you are back in that same paper with another essay about, of all things, Barbie's fiftieth anniversary, and somehow you also make that about Iranian America. You learned to interview your parents and dig up whatever they will give you from their past and add that to messy memories of your childhood and glue it all together. Be amazed at how your formula sometimes helps you work out some things; be amazed at how it sometimes seems to help others. Remind yourself that this can't last. Iranian-

Americans from all over the country write you and thank you, and you tell everyone this was a nice run—you did your part—and now you will go back to what you were meant to write: anything else.

4

Except you don't. You keep writing it. Tell yourself this is your new life every time an essay comes out in a venerable paper. Occasionally try to remind them you were a journalist before all this, a writer who wrote about music and art and fashion and books. Editors start asking for a collection of essays, but you think, *I've just begun.* Tell them in 2009, you're just entering your thirties, what do you know?

Know you're an essayist and know you can't back out now. During an interview someone asks you, *Why essays?* and you remind them you write fiction and they ask again, *Why essays?* and you joke about them finding you, and they ask again, *Why essays?* and you stumble on another answer: *service.* That somehow your people are not visible, these three decades of being in the United States, and people have needed you and while you can't speak for everyone, you can speak some part of this truth. *Service? Service.* Afterward, bum a few cigarettes the interviewer offers and smoke through a silence you did your best to create.

Start to wish other Iranian-Americans would write essays; even try to introduce the few who seem interested to editors, but the editors ask for more essays from you. How many essays can you write? you wonder, but every time one comes out, you start to see how they see it, and you see more. Step back from yourself and spin absolutely everything from the lens of Iranian Americana. An Iranian-American sensibility, an Iranian-American outfit, an Iranian-American state of mind, Iranian-American flora and fauna, an Iranian-American bowl of goddamn fruit. Watch yourself pitch the editor at the venerable publication an essay on the hit TV show *Thirtysomething*, a show you loved, and because in 2009, it's a big deal that it's out on DVD. Hear the editor in your head long before your real editor asks you if you can include your Iranian-American family in it, and catch yourself saying, *Yes, of course*, and do it, and never imagine years later you will teach that very own essay of yours as a mistake. Consider later that maybe you knew and didn't care; you knew the *service* and moreover you knew your function: you were not just writing Iranian America, maybe you were helping them create it.

Write a personal essay on the Persian New Year—that's what they want and that's what you deliver. By this point your parents know why you are asking them questions when you call; by this point they have gotten used to the fact that you will write about them and anything else Iranian America. When friends and family begin to marvel at all this, Miss Literary Iranian America, don't you deny it—smile and be grateful and lie that this is exactly what you dreamed of one day.

When another section editor of that same paper emails you, accept their request for a new essay, knowing that you can write an essay on absolutely anything for these people, provided it's about Iranian America—which it will be. Muslim reality TV the first time, Iranian reality TV the second time, *But we're big fans of your essays, so can you make it an essay not a review?* They want feelings, not facts, you know this by now. Write the first and write the second and duck all the love hurtling itself at you, a love you can't feel, a love you might fear.

Writing Iranian America turns out to have some downsides, but you think you know how to handle them. When Iranians write you and say you are not Iranian enough for them, thank them, and when others say you are too Iranian for them, thank them, too. Too pro-Islamic Republic and too royalist, too anti-Iranian and too nationalistic, too relatable and not relatable enough, maybe neocon and maybe communist. And where is your name from? Are you really Iranian? Why are you not married? Are both your parents really Iranian? Why do you say Iranian and not Persian? Why are you embarrassing us? Why are you not writing on subjects of a happier nature? Why are there so many jokes? What do you think of us? Are we good or bad? Are you good or bad? Why do you call us brown? Why do you not look more white? Why do you look so white? What god is your god? Why can't you write in a way I can understand? Why do you write at all? Why don't you stop writing? Why don't you stop smoking? When you get those messages, learn to let them say what they need to say. Occasionally engage, and often don't. *Service.*

Learn to live with hating yourself. Learn to live with hating Iranian America. Imagine the hell of dying in America while your parents envision the beauty of dying in Iran, and you wonder if there was ever anything in between for you.

5

When your editors leave the section where they first published you, think, *This is it*, what you've been waiting for—your run is over. Tell everyone you know it's been great, four years as an essayist of Iranian America! Imagine all topics you were supposed to write about, but you can't quite remember what they were. Try to remember and fail. *Hip-hop? White girls? Bars? Wars?* Try to remember and fail.

When, a few years later, a new editor at that venerable paper emails you, you pause at the first line. A pitch in the greeting, a story you know of: an Iranian band in Brooklyn has been the victim of a murder-suicide. For days you've considered reporting on this, thinking of the right venue, but they want a personal essay. "It seems to me like there might be something interesting to say, about the Iranian expat community, the American dream betrayed, or something along those lines." Think about her take for a moment and think about how you can't: how this story has nothing to do with assimilation. It is about a deranged person from your part of the world who shot some people from your part of the world, but it is much more about gun control and America and not about its dream being betrayed at all. Ask her if you can face America here, not just Iranian America, in the only piece you can write, pitch this to her and know the answer.

Remind yourself that you have been chronically ill for many years and buying cigarettes is no longer an option.

Write for other sections of that paper—the book review, where you sometimes wonder why they don't give you topics relating to Iranian America—until once again, in 2017, another section editor writes you, this time with a name that is definitely of Iranian America. When she says she wants a Persian New Year piece, a sweet nostalgia piece, remind her that four years ago, you wrote one.

Observe others writing about Iranian America. Encourage and amplify the many voices and viewpoints of your people, nearly four decades a minority in this America, with their own stories surfacing, too. Enjoy reading their accounts until readers warn you against your own enthusiasm. *I feel like they're ripping you off*, go messages from the concerned, and you don't know what to make of it. Against your better judgment, read more closely. Decide you will pretend not to notice. Pretend you are better than this competitive game they have set up for all of you to destroy yourselves in. Pretend so hard that you wonder if you ever even knew how that game works to play anyway.

Pretend to chain-smoke a couple of packs of cigarettes, killing hours in bottomless depression, and pretend Iranian America is all theirs, for whoever wants the wreckage.

6

Tell yourself this is the Last Essay, but remind yourself of all the other Last Essays. Wonder how much more of this you can take. Count that out of seventy pieces of nonfiction you've written since your first book came out in 2007; forty-eight have had to do with Iranian America. Ask yourself if it's too many or too few. Watch the news and marvel at how they obsessed over your country of origin, and continue to. Wonder if you and your family will end up in Muslim Camp after all. When people look at you with the pity and the regret again—*refugee, resident alien, political asylum seeker, immigrant, foreigner*—let them have it, and let yourself take it.

Write about it and make sure you keep writing about it. Plan out three more books and call it the end; each and every one is about Iranian America. Write all your secrets like every essay is a suicide note: one revealing that your Zoroastrian name is a fraud and you are a Muslim and watch everyone applaud it, people online and your own father, who gave you your name. Wonder if anyone is reading properly. Put "Iranian-American refugee" in your Twitter profile, the way all the other refugees are doing. Question if this is empowering. Imagine you've been throwing yourself off a cliff every time you've been writing, but it's hard to know if you are killing yourself or trying to fly. Wonder if a cliché like that is all you've got. Wonder if the death you've been imagining is just you becoming a bad writer.

Watch yourself making posts on Facebook and Twitter more than ever in 2017. Start asking white people to repost or echo the same sentiment so your ideas can get heard. Watch white Americans listen to one another but suddenly not be so sure about your words. Remind them that you know Iranian America and that they seemed to love reading you—quote your own pieces, send them the links, remind them they knew you—but watch them slowly back away. Watch other friends tell you it's not happening. Watch yourself worry about every word. Watch yourself apologize for things no one understands. Watch yourself think only in Farsi, like America never happened to you. Watch yourself burn out on the worry and remind yourself of where this essay started: begin by writing about anything else. *End by thinking about anything but yourself*, you tell yourself, but look at how you're all out of jokes.

7

Be a little astonished that there is another section of the Last Essay to write. Notice you've learned a few things about essays in this decade, that the ones you must write will write themselves for you. Remind yourself that when the performance is honest, two things happen: the essay will feel like it's killing you and the ending will not be what you thought it might be. Learn to respect more than resent planes of living and the rendering of living.

Note that you're not thinking about this when you read and then reread an email you receive late one night a few weeks after this first Persian New Year of the Trump administration, from an Iranian-American aspiring writer who tells you your work has saved her life, a woman twenty years your junior who asks if you have any words of advice. You thank her and feel embarrassed for your discomfort in reading her praise, and you try to channel her joy and enthusiasm and you fail, and you draft an email where you tell her to run, but don't say which way. *Run with everything you got, dear reader.*

Delete the email and start over, and watch weeks and weeks go by. One day open the draft and see the word *love*. Try to delete it, but it won't go away. Tell yourself your delete key is broken and get it fixed and still try. Tell yourself this happened for a reason—laugh at the audacity, the idiocy, the cliché—and one day, many years into a version of a future you might get, go as far as to grow into it again.

Thank you, the young woman writes. *I think I know what to do.*

You wait for more, but that's it.

Brown Album

At the bottom of everything there is the hallelujah.
—Clarice Lispector

This is the essay no one can touch.

This is the essay that wrote itself on Twitter for years, over the course of the decade I spent there sharing joys and anxieties with some people I knew but mostly people I didn't. This is the essay arising from the tweets that resulted in death threats. How many days did I kill there, hearing *Go Kill Yourself.* Some of those days coincided with days I thought that myself. And those were the days that this essay, like a worm, grew inside me until it could not be contained.

This is the essay that I wish to be unprintable, but instead to be scrawled in sky and dust and blood, in mitochondria and dander, anywhere but on the cold white page or in the equally hard white glare of the computer screen. I am writing this essay about whiteness from a human being many insist is white. This is the essay that many of my own people would tell me to go kill myself for because I deny the whiteness they claim. This is an essay that should be my manifesto: I deny our claims to whiteness. I want to remind those who can claim whiteness that they are a very small group. To survive our moment in 2020 and perhaps all the moments to come, we need to remind them who the real minorities are.

We are multiplying like blooms that push through the brambles. One hand chokes on the blood of the crimes of whiteness—some say these are the dry heaves of whiteness's last gasp—and the other hand flowers with all our mixes. Those who were once called "diverse people" are the majority of the world, who will never be erased.

This is the essay that says we are brown and we are everywhere. You can begin by seeing us and then attempting to love us, like we attempted to love you, in spite of that and that and that and that.

We move forward, but we forget nothing.

✳

My family had brown albums, literally. They were photo albums, and we were constantly taking photos. Our mirrors were often dirty, so I took selfies of myself, even at a young age. It took days, if not weeks, for the roll of film to become complete and for us to turn it in to the local Thrifty drugstore and have the photos developed. After receiving the little rectangles of paper, my mother immediately tucked them into the large brown albums she would buy at the local Pic 'N' Save. Every holiday when I came back from college, I would look at them and think: we exist. What I think I meant was that we survived.

※

In those brown albums, our family at times looks like a family and at other times not. My mother and father appear consistently. She, who passes for white, with European looks evoking Barbra Streisand or Sophia Loren, comes from Hamadan, the great Jewish center of Iran, where Queen Esther's tomb is located. I learned about this at a dinner with Iranians when a man I had never met before accused me of hiding that I was Jewish. I told him we have an aunt who converted to Judaism on my father's side, but if there were Jewish people on my mother's side, we had no idea. You don't talk about certain things when you are Iranian, and you could be me, more than four decades old, and know nothing of your family. Like my father—where are his people from?

I never forgot a gathering of my mother's relatives—again, all fair, freckled, all-American in their style—where a relative we barely knew joked about my father being African. Thirty years later I brought this up to my father and he didn't remember. I asked him more about where his family is from. So many of them, like his own father, are dark-skinned, tall, lanky—most closely resembling Barack Obama—and from a different world than my mother's. Because we struggle in person at times, never quite getting along, email is our refuge. At middle age, I ask him, finally, where he is from. We know his mother, who is also dark, lived in a small village called Garakan. But then he wrote:

My father's side lineage is more complicated. I hope one day I can do more research on that. Here is what I know:

1) Maybe about three hundred years ago: Khosrow Parsi, a Zoroastrian from India
2) Early nineteenth century: Mohammad Khan Baloch is a local ruler of Balochistan who rebelled against Fath-ali Shah Qajar and lost his life on that.

And there you go, my father has Afro-Iranian (Balochistan) and South Asian ancestry. The slave trade in Iran was strong until the mid-nineteenth century, when Arab slave traders sold black humans hailing from Southeast Africa. My father protested my trying Ancestry.com. I had been rejecting whiteness, the myth of Iranian Aryanness.

✳

In 2017, on the brink of 2018, I became ill with some unknown toxicity. The tests seem to indicate mold, but they also indicate all kinds of other factors. I should be incensed when doctors ask me if stress has played any role, but I can't lie. I tell them the truth. It delays my health care and only muddies the mystery. I have been unwell since 2016. Since the rainy day in New York when Trump won the election. If I am to be honest, maybe I wasn't well before, either. In 2011, there were reports over the local news in Leipzig that neo-Nazi activity had heightened. Brown shop owners disappeared. Hate crimes escalated in a country that had supposedly outlawed hate. I had spent the year on a fellowship in Leipzig, and my cab rides were filled with tension. I was in a country where I was seen as the new reviled minority: the Muslim. I started to get sick and sicker. I tried to ignore it and pitched a big investigative feature. I couldn't work on it. It later turned out that there was mold in that apartment, but there was also the trauma.

I interviewed a local cyber-watchdog group that was trying to combat the influence of the neo-Nazis. One told me the local Nazi clubhouse had Iranian flags on their tables. I asked why, and he said, *Ahmadinejad*, but I also supplied another answer after some thought: they thought we were the original Aryans. An ugly myth that occasionally my father talked about, with something like half-pride, when he felt Americans being racist—there it was again. A colleague took me to a punk show late in the year where most of the audience was composed of young men in jeans and shaved heads and tattoos, perhaps neo-Nazis. As he apologized to me, one young man came to talk to us. He claimed he had heard of me, as the local paper had done an article on me as a guest professor. He ran his tongue on my cheek and said, *Aryan goddess*. He walked away, laughing with the demonic smile you still see them wearing at rallies, because we now live in a country where it's happening, too, as I had feared. Who is safe and who is not?

In my final month teaching at Bard College—the end of a three-year visiting professorship—I am faced with an East Asian white supremacist in my first-year writing class. This student finds it okay to say hateful things about Jewish people and black people in confidence and eventually, as if to break me and my other students, in class. I break character and ask her to leave. I am no longer a professor but an opponent in a race war, and I want to tell her, What makes you think you are safe? She sends me harassing email after harassing email and again I break character and hurl the insults back. I tell someone I am dating that I don't think I am fit to teach anymore. He wonders if I am sick. But that's not it exactly. I mean, I am. But we all are. This country. This world. We are sick.

❋

Every Halloween, my mother and her mother wanted me to dress as Snow White. I was darker when I was a teenager, but both my mother and her mother felt confident I'd grow out of it. Stay out of the sun, my beloved grandmother would tell me; you don't want to become too brown. My aunt sewed me a perfect Snow White dress and I, browner and hairy and mustached, but forced into wearing red lipstick for the first time, wore that dress to school with misery. I looked nothing like Snow White, but the women in my family did not see that. They saw their dreams: skin as white as snow. In one of my brown albums, there was a photo of me clutching my black Cabbage Patch Kid doll, next to a Golden Books edition of *Snow White and the Seven Dwarfs*, with my mother at my side. As in many of our family photos, I don't look happy. But it's more than that. It almost looks like I was photoshopped in, like their dreams were photoshopped onto me.

Not long after Trump was elected, my father, whose politics swung from a love of Reagan to a love of Sanders, from conservative to socialist even, said to me at a dinner: "You should let go of some of your comments on race on social media." I wondered if it was because he was the only one in our family who was not securely an American citizen. I asked him, and instead he said something he'd never said, this man who taught me that we were *gandom-gan*: *We are Caucasians, face it.* My mother pleaded, *Not again, can't we have a nice dinner.* But we couldn't.

What if identity was always at the table? That was the rift that made us all impossibilities to one another. We had no origin stories but the ones we were given, the ones we choose of the ones we were given. You always want to be difficult, my father often said, and here it was again. All I could say at that dinner was something I've said too many times: but you were the one who taught us we weren't white in the first place. I don't stick around to hear his reply, because I can't bear it.

❋

On Christmas Eve 2017, I was unraveling, but I had work to do. I had a memoir in the process of being published that

I needed to finish edits on, another proposal to compose for this very book, parents to struggle with, bills to pay. I started pulling all-nighters. Usually the holidays were my favorite time—growing up, we had trees growing around us, and we reveled in the glitzy ostentation of Christmas even though we didn't celebrate it. This time I was in a dark place.

It didn't help that I had returned to Los Angeles just one week after teaching at my low-residency program to discover all sorts of horrors. First, it had been one of the more stressful teaching semesters I'd had in Vermont, only compounded by what was supposed to be a break just after but which instead turned into a stressful mini-vacation to Montreal, where my black boyfriend and I experienced what felt like all sorts of casual racism and xenophobia at every stop. "Not even Canada," I heard myself groan too many times. Something seemed off in the air of Glendale. Maybe it was the fires that had ravaged huge chunks of Southern California that season. But it was also the neighborhood.

On Christmas Eve morning, as I walked my dog along my parents' street, I saw parked on the street an old, badly battered Chevy Cheyenne pickup truck, the kind I would have loved to own once, covered in Confederate flags, on the back and on the front. I rushed in to ask my parents whose truck this was and they didn't know. More disturbingly, they suddenly seemed not to know what a Confederate flag was. Or did they ever? I was in shock.

I could have expected to see the sight in Mississippi, but in Los Angeles? Sure, this was the city that produced Stephen Miller and Steve Bannon, but when had the hatred hit home so literally for me? I forced it into the back of my head. I was hiding in my room, writing and editing feverishly and wishing I were doing anything else. My boyfriend, who lived at the other end of the state, had promised me a delivery that day, so I was looking forward to receiving some flowers. Around mid-afternoon, he texted me, asking me to go outside. *Hurry*, he texted, and I dashed to the front door, only to find *him* standing there. There he was with his beautiful smile, holding a gift, open arms, ready for me. I began crying like a pageant queen. No one had ever done something so romantic for me before. I had assumed he was occupied with his kids in Oakland, but he had split the day for his loved ones.

As I went to go get into his rental car, I took in the scene. There he was smiling, gift in hand, open arms, his rental truck, directly in front of the pickup with the Confederate flags. In the car, I told him to be discreet—I was horrified the owner could see us—and to drive around the dead end and up to the car to see the stickers. He did and began laughing. *Fucking Glendale*, he said. He was from Southern California, too. Back in the eighties, you heard about Armenian gangs beating up on Mexican and black gangs. The Armenian Glendale PD was notoriously racist. I wondered why I was surprised then.

We ate dinner and checked into a hotel. I could not stop obsessing over the sight of my black boyfriend next to a pickup truck with Confederate flags, in front of the building where my Iranian family lived, apparently oblivious to what a Confederate flag meant. It was too much.

I didn't sleep that night. It had to do with feeling in danger and being afraid, I guessed. It was about America. No, it was about this America. Maybe, this was the America it had been all along when I wasn't looking.

❋

In winter 2017, I tweeted "one of the top 100 most exhausting things about white people is their obsession with joan didion."

I have read Didion my whole life, and have been told I should worship Didion my whole life. I remember the first time an old professor of mine tried to introduce me to the New York literary world's finest, at the old Elaine's. That evening a writer whose name I didn't know asked me where I was from and after hearing the long story said, "Well, so like an Iranian Didion! L.A. to New York to L.A. to New York! A real city girl, then?" I didn't know what to say. I was eighteen.

The summer before, I had read Didion the way I had as a child read *Tales from Shakespeare* by Charles and Mary Lamb: because I knew I should. And because I was told it would help me fit into New York. I also thought it might make me understand Los Angeles more, but I didn't find my Los Angeles in her pages: Alhambra, Monterey Park, and Pasadena were missing; the brown and black kids were missing. I could not find myself. Her tone, classically ice-cold, crisp, detached, precise, immaculate naturally—she was everything I could not be and was not. English was my second language and I was infatuated with Southern writers and their twists and tangles. Their biblical intonations and invocations were rooted in my part of the world. They were messy, they un-

derstood conflict, they understood injustice and loss and guilt
and shame and horror. Didion observed it all from a distance,
I felt, in a chic dress, cigarette in hand, perfect hair and sunglasses.

I taught Didion for years. My students loved her, and
I understood why. In my dozen or so years of teaching I
taught mostly white kids at elite liberal arts schools, and if
I wanted to score points with them, I taught Didion, James
Salter, John Cheever. WASPs love a WASP story, though they
might not admit it. Then I'd toss James Baldwin at them and
there would be long silences, punctuated by comments from
students who'd suddenly had a breakthrough.

I hate being white, a male freshman once told me in confidence.

I laughed.

Do you? he asked.

I'm not white, I said.

I don't understand, he said.

I can't remember if I explained or not.

In any case, I continued to teach Didion.

I watched the Didion documentary, and I don't know
if that's what inspired it, but perhaps it left me feeling cold
about her. How badly I want to love her the way everyone
else does, I thought as I watched. Instead, she was an American I did not have access to, no matter how many WASPy
New York gatherings or L.A. bonfires I'd hung out on the
fringes of.

I tweeted about her. Students from the low-residency
MFA program I had just started teaching at started a thread

on their Facebook group, and ultimately reported me to the program director, a few even claiming that with my opinion of Didion, I should not be allowed to teach.

I was then also teaching at another low-residency program in Vermont, where almost all my students were white, too. I didn't know how to make a teaching moment out of this. I responded on Facebook to say that I am allowed to have opinions on books and writers, that I have strong opinions and make jokes, and I also have the freedom to poke at white culture.

In the end, I did not get fired. My brown friends and black boyfriend eventually were able to laugh about this episode, but I never got over it. I did one more residency at that school in Maine before I became ill again. There, white students apologized to me, often drunkenly.

Secretly, I had nightmares about this incident for months. I had never gotten in trouble as an adult before, certainly not for my teaching. But in my nightmare, I saw me, in my usual budget-bought "shabby chic," as one student called my style, hair in knots, wobbling on my cane, and then I saw her: Didion, eternally in a summer of '69, smoking away, thin but not from illness like me, hair in perfect golden waves, shaking her head. You don't cross Didion.

❋

Months later, it was my birthday and my boyfriend and I were sitting together in a Persian restaurant. We were celebrating my fortieth and the fact that a publisher took on this book. I over-ordered everything and we laughed at the mess of riches. The waiter talked only to him, knowing he is not Iranian like I am.

We were both exhausted, him from his new journalism assignments, me from working on the edits on the book published before this one. As it sometimes happens with love, something turned wrong, and this ended up being our last meal together. We broke up. Just like that. After months of bliss, it was over.

As he drove me home, I could not stop crying. This was the best relationship of my adult life. We had made plans for the future together. Our breakup didn't make sense to me. I played in my mind that it would pass, we were both stressed, but by the time we got to my parents' Glendale apartment and to the truck with the stickers of the Confederate flag parked right in front the building, it really seemed over. I gave him a bracelet he had given me—something he had bought on a field trip in eighth grade for his dream girl, which apparently was me, which his white foster mother had found in her basement, untouched. He didn't want it back, but I knew it was over, and to look at it again was going to kill me.

I don't remember how we said goodbye, but I know it was probably angrier than we both wished. There was no kiss, and there was no hope. What I do remember is his saying he had to stop and get gas, and my calling him minutes after he sped off to make sure he did not do it in Glendale, and his saying, almost with a dead chuckle, "Of course I won't stop for gas in Glendale. You think I forgot I was black?"

❋

Half a year later, what feels like a lifetime, I see the owner of the truck: a white woman. Short, middle-aged, capris, sneakers, someone's boring aunt. She shuffles through something in the back, and I, thinking of all the other bumper stickers, wonder if it is for a gun. I imagine her saying *Trump's America, bitch*, to me as she walks by. Then I think, *There is no way she will walk by.* She saw that I saw her. No one else I had spoken to in the neighborhood had seen the owner of the truck before. We made eye contact.

She does walk by, and as she passes, she looks at me and I decided to hold my stare, too. And of all gestures, what I get is a nod. I nod back, no idea what that means, except that she was maybe smiling, too—hard to tell—and then I wonder if she thought I was white.

And I think back to every moment in my life when I wondered if someone thought I was white.

You are obsessed with race, a college boyfriend told me, 1996, the day after we stormed the president's house over issues of diversity being grossly ignored. I remember I had nodded. You bet I am.

We are *gandom-gan*, my father told me when I was as young as I can remember, which means wheat-colored, the equivalent of brown in Farsi. He had told me that so many times when I struggled to fill out the bubbles that asked to identify my race. He recommended I put Asian. Usually I checked Other and then filled in Middle Eastern. Now Middle Eastern is becoming a parenthetical for Caucasian. I feel paralyzed.

They want us to be white. Like those Nazis, they want to claim us. Maybe some of us wanted to claim that identity, too.

I saw a long thread on Twitter that nearly went viral of an Iranian girl asking "are Persians white y/n" and the answers were a mess of everything from sincerity ("depends on how *you* identify," "depends on what region your family comes from") to ridicule ("are Persians Iranian y/n") to downright racism ("Persians are sandniggaz bitch"). She deleted her tweet and maybe her account, but I remember laughing and fuming and eventually crying.

✳

Why do you insist on rejecting our whiteness, an anonymous Twitter account wrote me once. *I am Iranian, and you make me ashamed.*

I blocked him as I had finally learned.

I wanted to write him to tell him that I am obsessed with race. Have you not noticed?

In my defense, we lived in America. I could have written, *Have you not looked around?*

✳

Before we broke up, my boyfriend and I listened to the news that another black teenager had been shot indiscriminately and discussed how a civil war may happen again. Black against white? we both wonder. Rich against poor? Trump's America, bitch, and it's hard to know.

But one thing we do know is that we have no idea where

the brown people will fall in all this, because there is no *one* brown people. There is no *one* white or black people, either, but at times I felt like brown included most of the others. Where was the solidarity? But what solidarity? My first boy-friend, Mexican, hated visiting Puerto Rican New York. It reminded me of how every country in the Middle East has a bone to pick with the countries next door. Solidarity is per-haps impossible for the brown people of this earth.

Maybe there is no such thing as a brown person anyway. *Gandom-gan*, wheat. I think of teaching my students about colorism and what it means to be light-skinned in the context of literature. I wonder if they would carry it out with them.

A day after hearing about the dead black teenager, I argue with my father about whether racism originated in our be-loved Middle East, cradle of civilization. Where did the black people of Bandar Abbas, on the southern coast of Iran, come from? He laughs it off.

Why do you want to hate us? he asks me.

I don't, I say. It's because I love us. I think of Baldwin: *I love America more than any other country in this world, and, exactly for this reason, I insist on the right to criticize her perpetually.*

All I know is we have to do something. Someone is re-sponsible. Maybe we all are. *I was gripped by panic during those Trump years,* I imagine I will say someday if we live to see our way through them.

❋

I am obsessed with race, but in my defense, again, racists flock to me. For a while I thought it was just because I "pass."

Perhaps they see it as a betrayal, this white-looking girl who won't claim her whiteness. But these days I don't know what it is. It seem racists are looking for anything to stick to.

In Santa Fe, a man I trusted, who was helping me look for mold-free housing when I was at my sickest, used the words *camel jockey* with me. He said the problem with homes and mold is "all those carpets the camel jockeys bring here and sell to us." I asked him does he realize who he is talking to, where I am from? "Well, no offense, but you know what I mean," he said. I don't talk to him again, but it was with tears in my eyes, weeks later, that I asked my mother to roll up the Persian carpets in their moldy condo, and she didn't understand why it made me cry, and I could no longer explain myself.

In Santa Fe, a woman whose husband had an InfoWars sticker on his SUV let me stay with them for a while. They were both sick themselves, but they had resources and they could help me, they said. They seemed kind, but every day the husband brought up Iran, wanted to know more about Iran. "They don't want to kill us, do they?" I had to reassure him, but somehow it was always a sort of small talk for us. He supported Trump, thought he was misunderstood. When his wife was out of town, he showed me videos of alien conspiracy theories, of the new world order, the depopulation agenda and California, and chemtrails. "I wouldn't be surprised if we all have chemtrail flu," he said, which of course I tried to research and gave more time to than it deserved. Every day he pointed at the lines in the sky and said, "No wonder we feel like shit. You know who wants to stop that? Trump. You know who loved that stuff? Obama." I endured this for weeks and weeks on end until, a few days before Christmas, they kicked me out. Another sick friend was moving in, a friend with cancer, they said, but I think they couldn't handle the few times I let my opinions leak out.

A few months later, I found myself staying with another couple, this time in a suburb of San Francisco. This time they were liberals, people who also knew chronic pain and who had an empty room in their home. The first weeks were blissful and joyous, and I felt I was part of their family. I managed to wind up and down the streets of their town, invigorated by the ocean air. But things went awry one night during the third week. I was feeling particularly sick, as I always did, and the truth was that I did not want to talk. The woman of the house had had a few drinks and suddenly she was raging at me. I had upset her and I didn't know why. I assumed it was because I was sick and sometimes didn't want to talk, and if I did, my talking was about sickness, which no one wanted to hear, really. But this was about something else.

She had heard me complain about California and California health care, and she had had it, she told me. She was a socialist, she said, and that's the closest we had. I tell her that, for my disease, California has not worked well. I have become sicker and sicker. I tell her that MassHealth, from what I have read, seems closer to the socialism she likes. But it became an argument. I watched the liquid in her glass (since becoming sober a few years earlier, I'd taken to closely watching the drinking habits of angry people). She was screaming, and then I found myself saying, "I'm sorry. I promised myself long ago I would not allow white people to rage at me. And especially not now. Not in this America. It's too much." I walked away and went to my room, which of course was her room—I was the "guest" here—and she came in crying, upset over what happened between us. I told her to just let it go. "I can't believe you called me a white woman. I can't believe you think I am a racist." I told her I never said that, but she insisted. Again I told her I never said that, but again she insisted.

I left. Weeks later, an Iranian woman I didn't know who heard I had to leave helped me carry my stuff out of their home. This woman was chronically ill and in bad shape but said we Iranians are family, and I felt it deeply. There were mudslides all around town; her car got stuck on the driveway and a friendly guy had to dig us out. That night she drove me to a hotel an hour away, near my temporary doctor's office, where they gave me discounts, seeing how disabled I was.

She was quiet for most of the ride, which made sense to me—we barely knew each other—but when she said, "They've lost their minds," I knew exactly what she meant.

And then, many months later, still without a home, a couple reached out to me on Facebook. By then I should've known not to trust couples, but I still did somehow. I was staying at my parents' house again, and the mold in it was making me more disabled. I was also stressing them out, so I needed a new idea. This couple was also inside my demographic— disabled, too. Like me, they were mold refugees of sorts, so they could relate, they said, having moved to a high-rise in the middle of L.A. after years of living with black mold in the Northwest.

For nearly a month it worked out. I slept with three pets—including my own dog, which was bliss, as we'd been estranged for months—in their living room. It really seemed like it could work. We were a team, we joked, and even as we kept different hours and dealt with different health problems, we seemed a pack, like the animals. We even dreamed of moving to New York together. One day amidst the couple's discussion about a rare outing—a brunch—there was tension; it came out that they had a problem with my being there. The husband pulled me aside later and said they were worried about me, that I was anorexic or bulimic, that I reminded them of their friend who committed suicide. Their friend had Lyme disease.

I didn't know what to say. He was going on about their hardships, which I used to understand as another chronically ill person, but this was about his salary. He made only six figures and it wasn't enough for his wife, so going to a fancy brunch needed to be part of their lifestyle. He felt I had judged them. He wondered if it was a good idea for me to stay.

"I don't know what you are talking about," I finally said, exhausted, amazed I had trusted yet another couple who took me in for a while. What did these couples have in common other than some illness? Not much. But then of course I knew it: whiteness. I wanted to bite my tongue, but then it came rolling out: "But the most white-privilege thing I have ever heard of—it's almost funny—is getting kicked out over brunch."

I almost wanted to laugh, except I was homeless again.

The next morning, as my mother came to deliver me some soups, the wife pulled her aside and said again that they were worried about me and suicide and that I called her husband a racist.

"When did I do that?"

He clarified that I said *white privilege*.

"Why do you even assume I am white?" said the white woman.

I had an answer for that, but I was already out the door.

✳

When I was a child, I loved Glendale, California. There was a mall there that I worshipped—it was infinitely bigger than our local mall. By the time I was sixteen, I turned on it, and it became the site of migraines and fainting episodes and panic attacks. My father noticed years later that a sign there mentioned that there might be cancer-causing chemicals inside, but, of course, such a notice was the kind of thing you ignored if Californian—what *didn't* have a label that warned you of cancer?

What I didn't know about, until long after my parents' move there in 2011 and the Christmas I saw the truck with the Confederate flag, was that Glendale historically was also a hotbed of racist activity.

A friend twenty years my senior told me there were swastikas on the lampposts, but assuaged me by saying it was either an "Indian or Hopi thing, I'm pretty sure."

Glendale had been one of L.A.'s whitest neighborhoods—a 1996 *Los Angeles Times* article reports that in the late fifties it was 97 percent white. The Forest Lawn cemetery, Glendale's most famous landmark, allowed only white people to be buried there. The commander of the American

Nazi Party's Western Division lived there in the mid-1960s; so did the head of California Ku Klux Klan.

The same article from 1996 mentions:

> Five years ago, Nestle International moved to
> Glendale from the mid-Wilshire district. Members
> of the company's black-employee association voiced
> their concerns about the city's racist reputation.
> City officials met with Nestle executives to assure
> them that all their employees would be treated fairly.
> Since the move, some of these black employees have
> decided to live in the city.

I wished for more articles such as this one. Everyone I asked in Glendale, including a prominent black journalist who had recently moved there, told me that they had no idea. My parents will never move. Their building, what they call a "sick building"—ironically where I put the final touches on my memoir, *Sick*, and where I grew sicker than ever—is full of mold and pesticides, but my parents like it there.

They ignore me when I bring up the Confederate flag out front, or they give me the old immigrant line: *They don't bother us; we don't bother them.*

I am stirring the pot.

Trump's America, bitch, and if you don't like it you can leave.

But leave to where?

I become suicidal that year again, and therapists ask me why I talk whiteness when I talk to them about my illness.

Meanwhile, growing more enfeebled, I also grow whiter and whiter in shade, like the joke's on me.

✻

Let the record state that, during Trump's America, I became broken.

I, a brown woman, forever brown, broke.

Something in me, something far above me, knows I will mend.

We will get through this, say the voices of ancestors.

I might never go back, but I know they will live in the brown albums that still exist in my parents' home, one on top of the other, full of dust, for as far as I know, I was the only one who looked at them, year after year, to understand what had become of us.

Acknowledgments

Generally my acknowledgments sections have been very long, but these days as the United States considers war with Iran yet again, as the halves of my hyphen seem irreparably split once more, I find myself with fewer words.

I want to thank my family and friends. Their patience and understanding gave me the courage to tell the stories that were often theirs.

I want to thank my surreally hardworking agent, Seth Fishman; my brilliant, big-hearted editor, Maria Goldverg; and the whole Knopf Doubleday family for being class acts all the way through. Robin Desser believed in my essays back in 2011, long before I dared call myself an essayist; that was the first time I even let myself imagine a book like this.

I want to thank my editors at *The New York Times* in particular, who put me and my work, as they say, truly on the map. All the editors I worked with for the essays in this book were heroic in handling somewhat uncharted waters: Mark Lotto, David Shipley, Stephanie Goodman, Deb Olin Unferth, Tim Parsa, Sari Botton, Don George, Grant Jarrett, Sarah Hepola, Maggie Bullock, Stephen Pierson, Manjula Martin, Jamison Stoltz, Viet Thanh Nguyen, Jane Carr, John Freeman, Ky Henderson, and Mensah Demary.

I want to thank most of all Iranians, in Iran and in the diaspora. I would be nothing without you.